TAKING THE
ONE SEAT

JOHN M. TRAVIS

FOREWORD BY JACK KORNFIELD

EDITED BY COY F. CROSS II, PH.D.

Koho Pono, LLC

Taking the One Seat

Published by Koho Pono, LLC
Clackamas, Oregon USA; https://KohoPono.com

First Paperback Edition 14April2019

ISBN: 978-1-938282-28-7 (trade paper)
ISBN: 978-1-938282-29-4 (ebook)

Foreword by Jack Kornfield
Edited by Coy F. Cross II, Ph.D

DEDICATION

This book is dedicated to Anagarika Munidra, S.N. Goenka, Ajahn Chah, and the 16th Karmapa.

I also dedicate this book to the Travis clan: Tai, Pema, Tenzin, Myla, Kian and their children.

And to the "Mountain Stream community" I dedicate this book.

TABLE OF CONTENTS

FOREWORD

"John Travis brings fifty years of contemplative practice alive in the transformative words of this book. He has explored the *Dharma* in many forms: as a wandering holy sadhu in India, a dauntless yogi and courageous spiritual adventurer, as a poet and a meditator, as a student of a hundred spiritual teachers and as a beloved teacher himself, a father and grandfather and community builder and all along a lover of the Path of the Heart.

These many facets of John's life are woven into the beautiful and deep teachings you will find here. In *Taking the One Seat* you can hear John urging you to look at the truth of life from a vast perspective, and to tend your life with exquisite mindful care. John wants you to remember your True Nature, to discover within your own heart a timeless inner peace and happiness, a graciousness amidst all the changing conditions of the world. This is an invitation to awaken. Offering this truth and the practices of how to do so are the essence of this new work.

Just as Buddhist texts begin with the words "Oh Nobly Born, you who are the sons and daughters of the Awakened ones, remember who you really are." John's words can remind you, you are consciousness itself. Born in you is the potential for liberation, ease, and a great heart of compassion, wide enough to hold all the world.

John does not teach these truths from a linear mind. As a poet, his teachings unfold like the Ganges, one river with a myriad of voices, becoming many streams in the delta, always open, graceful from its first plunge in the Himalayas until pouring into the vast ocean below. The teachings of *Taking the One Seat* are similarly open, timeless, inviting you to enter this stream of awakening, and see for yourself.

From his years of practice and training John's voice offers his readers reassurance, and he counsels trust and perseverance. He knows first hand that liberation is possible. And he wants you to join him in this marvelous journey.

Reading a *Dharma* book is a meditation practice.

While it offers reassurance and inspiration, teachings and practices, it asks for your perseverance and willingness to practice. It reminds you to plant seeds of mindfulness and compassion and to trust in your growing capacity to live with a free heart.

Read these pages slowly, savor them.

Take the particular teachings that most touch you as medicine, as jewels, as an invitation to live with love and joy amidst it all.

May this book be a blessing to which I add my own.

Metta,

Jack Kornfield

Spirit Rock Center

2019

The following chapters were first presented as John M. Travis's *Dharma* talks at retreats over the last several years.

CHAPTER ONE

CALMING THE MUDDY WATER

So this is the great distraction from your own body, your own mind, and that space that I get to fill for a short time before you go back to your own garbage. I would like to start with a poem:

First Day

Like a great blazing fire, body came to rest on the cushions,
fired up to stay awake and present,
only to find bitter-sweet drifting off,
old stories holding court,
while body cried out, "Pay attention to me, I'm the most important."
Everybody, everybody, demanding attention.
Nobody getting first place today.
Maybe enlightenment can wait.
Where are my car keys?

During this first day there is a lot of drifting off. This is the nature of the mind, sleepiness, discomfort. It's like a swamp that you're trying to get through. It's somebody's idea that somehow you'll be better next time.

1

The truth is that on this first day a lot is being asked of you. It's a very simple thing called self-acceptance. The more we struggle and try to fight against it, the more it causes us difficulty and problems. It's the way it is!

Another aspect, like self-acceptance, is self-compassion. You come here seeking techniques and "carrot in front of the horse" ideas about awakening and enlightenment. It's good stuff. But, it's also about your ability to stay present, sometimes in the midst of your internal dialogue and chaos.

I often joke about this. For so many years I taught in big venues with Jack Kornfield. There would be three or four teachers on the podium. As soon as Jack began to talk, I fell asleep. His voice was so melodious and so nice, I would just crash. I did this for many years. Jack was always very kind about it. I heard the first 3-5 words of his talks and that was the end of it.

Over the years I began to recognize that it wasn't that I didn't want to hear him and I finally figured out how to work with it. I had come out of the Burmese tradition that said, "All you need is four hours of sleep a night." I had this warrior part of me that said, "That's okay, everything will be fine." But as soon as everything calmed down, over I went. I never fell off the stage by the way. I never hit my nose on the stage either, but I came pretty close a few times.

I stopped falling asleep after I learned self-acceptance and then self-compassion. At the time I didn't realize there was such a thing as sleep-deprivation. Four hours sleep was not enough for me to function in this culture. If you live in the forest areas of Burma, there isn't the tension we're accustomed to in the West. I'm very sensitive. I pick up a lot from my environment. I used to get anxious with it, but now I don't so much. But I remember it takes its toll after a while.

You are going to get through this. It's going to be fine. A lot of you come out of a very hectic environment and there is a lot of busyness that goes on in your head. You don't have to go looking for it, it comes to you.

I love the story about the monk who was always falling asleep and the great Zen master. The master's assistant kept admonishing the monk. The Zen master commented, "Oh, I wish I could just put his head in my lap and let him sleep."

I think there is something to that. When the person is rested, the practice will do itself. It's not necessary to berate yourself about that. I'm not going to say, "Don't try to stay awake." But do it in a way that recognizes this is about a balanced way of holding this stuff.

We are so affected by the outside world. We are constantly reacting to all the stimulus presented to us. As a culture, I think we are incredibly sensitive. You may not believe that. But at least the people who come to the retreats that I have been doing for the past fifty years are incredibly sensitive people. They come to these retreats on a timeline, so they think, "Maybe I can get awakened faster." From here I say, "No."

This is an invitation to your internal world. You bring to the retreat a lot of the same stimuli that you had from the outside. Your internal world is like the ocean. It doesn't just suddenly settle down; there are waves that keep coming. But because of the restraint or renunciation that happens here, by nature they begin to settle down or slow down. Then there is this incredible invitation to the intimacy of our lives, of who we are. The waves will, in a sense, calm down.

I used to think that if I tried harder, particularly on the first day, things would be better. "Oh, I remember, if you put as much effort as you can right at the beginning, then it will be okay." I was good at that. I did that a lot.

Then maybe I got old. Suddenly, I realized, "If it's really about this middle way, this balance, there will be a backlash to all this effort." My whole process was about getting high, somehow pushing my practice to a point where it was transcendent, but it had a backlash to it.

I encourage you to naturally allow yourself to move into this. We are moving into this intimacy of who we are. Who we are appears to be true, but that is not actually so. We have to allow the waves to calm down. There is a Chinese saying, "Don't stir muddy water." You have to think about that for a minute. If you want to see clearly, this practice is very much about not adding anything. In our culture, we are constantly stirring the muddy water expecting to see more clearly. That is not how it works.

One of the beauties of coming together like this with this collective intention, we all have one nature, we are all going to settle. As we calm, the particles in the muddy water will begin to settle. Letting the particles settle is the invitation to the intimacy of this remarkable truth, this privilege of being here. It's amazing to recognize the truth of your body that you drive around with your thinking and your planning. You don't listen very well. You drive it and it follows direction. But there is this incredible mystery, I am just amazed.

There are the histamines the liver produces against toxins. Toxins come into our bodies and our bodies, as much as they can, purify the processes to avoid reactions. There are so many functional pieces of our bodies that it takes a couple of days here to settle the waves and particles.

I love this quote from the Venerable Ajahn Chah, "Do everything with the mind that lets go. Do not expect any praise or reward. If you let go a little, you'll have a little peace. If you let go a lot, you'll have a lot of peace. If you let go completely, you'll have complete peace and freedom, your struggle with the world will have come to an end." To practice in that way is directly associated with our capacity to have this intimacy, to feel into how we breathe, how our body feels itself. Our bodies can drag along stuff from the past few days or weeks or even childhood. The practice here will help keep things in balance.

When I went to India in the '60s I loved the custom of bowing. When we came back to the West, we didn't do that. We didn't have Buddhas here either, it was just the teachings. Now we have all sorts of paraphernalia. Ultimately, part of it's the humility, but the other part is honoring what it is that appears. If we could bow to all our discomforts and to all our old stories and say, "Hi,

I'm glad you came. Please take a seat. I'm not here to kick you out. I'm here to have a relationship with you." I think this would help take some of the power away from our discomfort. When the power is taken away, then that which is holding court begins to settle down. It's not such a problem. It's just another path.

Things go through my mind like everyone here. I was thinking, "I have had heroes, including a remarkable couple I met in India."

When I was probably twenty-four I had been a couple of years in India and occasionally I encountered some phenomenal people. Then I met a couple in their forties. They had been with R.D. Laing in the early 1960s. The woman was the most remarkable person I had ever known. They had a home in Great Britain, which they rented out and spent the next five years driving a Land Rover to India. He was a poet and she was this powerful lady. I was really humbled by them. She had been a flamenco dancer in Spain and a potter. Then she got involved in the whole R.D. Laing, psychiatry, rebirthing, and LSD experience. The man had left the U.S. in the 1960s because of the Vietnam War and never returned to the States. If I remember correctly, they broke down in the Hunza Valley in Pakistan. It took three months to get the parts they needed to start moving again. I thought, "Oh, if I could just have the patience to do something like that." I didn't have much patience at all then. They had made it to India, and after a retreat they picked me up and I drove with them up into the mountains. We rented a house up this riverbed. They did self-retreats up there. I think he ended up living in Norway, where he wrote books on Shamanism. They died in their sixties. I always thought, "If I could just be that kind of Gypsy!"

They were great teachers. They inspired me to discover the *Dharma* through the right life-style. I learned, "It's not about the circumstances we experience; it's about our ability to accept and be with whatever comes into our lives."

I want to share this R.D. Laing quote from them, "The range of what you think and do is limited by what you fail to notice. Because you fail to notice that you fail to notice, there is little that you can do until you notice that failing to notice shapes our thoughts and deeds."

I've had a lot of really fine teachers. We find incredible people who motivate us in different ways. I think we all have people who have turned us on to the *Dhamma*. They inspire us to become who and how we are.

Usually at the winter retreats in Asia, people come from all over the world. I heard this story from someone else, but it's a great story. One of my teachers had a very heavy Indian accent and you had to adjust to his voice. On the first night, a person went in for the instructions. What he heard was: "Observe your desperation!" He spent all night observing his desperation, until the instructions the next morning when the teacher repeated, "Observe your respiration!" But "observe your desperation" was a very profound instruction for starting a retreat. Observe *your* desperation and see how it happens.

So you come to a retreat and parts of you are standing straight up, on high alert, and these parts get caught on something. It's like a roulette wheel, you spin it and it gets caught on something. You aren't caught yet, and that is good. Particles begin to settle, and as they begin to settle, and you take part in your practices, you see the amount of activity that you're embodying. It's neither good nor bad. It's just seeing how it's nipping at your operating system. This is a burden of the human condition. As Zen Master Dogen noted, "To study the self is to know the self. To know the self is to release the self. To release the self is to open to the whole world."

Essentially, we are creatures whose view is like a horse with blinders. The process of letting everything settle is to pull the blinders back, just a little bit at a time. That's why we call it "insight practice". It's based on the ability to understand without forcing it. Ultimately, there is no way of achieving this through striving; it's just a way of being and holding. It begins to open a little bit. Then later it opens a little bit more. Then there is some sense of connection. I think sometimes it's simply not being caught in the past or the future, but being in what is available to you. And what is available to you and what is a lot of this is just a body sensation. You live in this moment and there is a phenomenal intelligence that begins to recognize that it has the power to let go. Ultimately, it's the lining up of the body, the heart, and the mind. I say "line up" in that there is a sense of relaxation, a sense of "you know, it's okay. I actually have this power of being at ease and having this sense of peace". It's not about the circumstances.

In our time here, if you can learn just a little bit of this, it will be helpful. There are going to be a lot of shocks that come along and things you are not going to like. You have the ability to recognize that they do have power, and we are wired into first reaction, but this practice is teaching us another thing. It's the ability to feel our first reaction, to know it, and to recognize that it doesn't have to be bad in its entirety. That is a gift. That is a tremendous gift, because it's the beginning of the capacity to "step into the fire and not be burned". I think this is based on that. "Can I teach myself that even when things are bad, I don't have to burn with it?"

These are simple things here. It's really the practice of sitting in the stillness and allowing things to come and go. Ultimately, there is a process of turning our attention to opening that part in us that is closed. If we can just do that. "Oh, here is that contraction that I feel, or that expectation that I have." If you could at that moment see that you have the power to not contract, to open to what you're closed to, you can choose a different path.

There is also an art to balancing. The balancing has to do with noticing that just as we are opening to what is closed, we are also reactive. Our practice is how, in the reactivity, do we find our equanimity, our balance, and our way of letting it open instead of closing down around it. It's finding that you have the power to balance your emotional reactivity and experience this.

Another aspect of this is similar to self-acceptance and self-compassion. Once the mind starts to settle down, we can explore what is underneath the surface, what is hidden from us. There is the art of being open to what we have shut down or closed around and finding the balance in our reactivity to our memories, our thoughts, our wants, and our desires. That is the practice: to explore.

This is all simply based on the Four Noble Truths, the fundamentals. A Western approach is to recognize that there is a problem, which is the First Noble Truth.

Then we see there is a way to diagnose the problem, which is simply to explore how we cling or attach to things. This is the Second Noble Truth.

There is a prognosis, the Third Noble Truth. The prognosis comes after we have taught ourselves internally how not to suffer and to recognize the nature of attachment. This is what the Buddha called *nibbana*. Maybe that word is too big, because we make ideals of that. Maybe it's simply we have "non-disturbing" awareness. Like, "Oh, it's okay." Suddenly the world is not what it was.

The Fourth Noble Truth, "The Path", is in many ways "the treatment". So we have the problem, the diagnosis, the prognosis, and the treatment. This is the medicine.

Everything we are doing here has been going on for 2,550 years - actually, a lot longer than that. People went and sat down. Sometimes they had concise instructions. Other times they were told, "Sit there. You will be okay. You just have to untangle your tangles." If you can do that and see how you do that, then the idea of freedom and peace and ease are truly at your fingertips.

I'll just end with reading this again:

First Day

Like a great blazing fire, body came to rest on the cushions,
fired up to stay awake and present,
only to find bitter-sweet drifting off,
old stories holding court,
while body cried out, "Pay attention to me, I'm the most important."
Everybody, everybody, demanding attention.
Nobody getting first place today.
Maybe enlightenment can wait.
Where are my car keys?

CHAPTER TWO

OWNING ALL OF OURSELVES

Out of the Mess

The wind whistling through this body,
maybe it could blow the many thoughts,
stories and feelings out through the mountains,
scattering them for miles and miles.
But today, sitting on this sore bum, knees a little creaky,
not sure why I would want to inhabit this ignored body,
difficult pulling buoyant mind down,
down into this skittish body,
staying only a moment, then off again,
prancing around,
hoping to think myself out of all these discomforts,
but remembering this sacred and enchanted place,
asking only to surrender the body,
stepping into its own natural loveliness,
body inhabiting body.
Awareness has the home destined to feel itself, one breath
at a time,
making nothing out of all of this, resting in its totality,
body in body.

I'll start with an old, old Chinese story:

Two young children, Singi and Ochu, were friends and they played together all the time, went to school together, and hung out. They grew up together. Even their dads said, "You get along so well, it would be nice if you married."

The children took that to heart, particularly Ochu. The culture of that time was about arranged marriages with the father deciding what was best for the family system.

So Singi's father chose a different man for his daughter to marry, not Ochu. Ochu was totally distraught. They lived on a river, so he stole a boat and began to sail downstream. Then Singi came out of the bushes and hailed him. They left their village and settled in a different village, downstream. They lived and worked there and had two children. But they were disturbed by how this had all come about. Five years passed and they decided they would return to their village and ask forgiveness from her father.

So they returned upstream to their village. Ochu went to Singi's father and asked for forgiveness. The father asked, "Why? Singi's in her room and has not come out in five years."

Ochu said, "No. She is down in the boat and you

now have two lovely grandchildren."

The father didn't believe him and sent his servant down to check. Sure enough, there was Singi with the two children. The servant came back and told her father. The father, in wonder, went into his daughter's room and told her what was happening. Then father and daughter went down to the river to see for themselves. As the daughter and the young mother approach each other they hug. And as they hugged, they became one.

In our Western culture, this is an imperative talk, simply due to the reality of our cultural truth. Like this Chinese story, many of us have lived divided lives. We have abandoned part of ourselves.

When we are young we are whole. "Awareness" has always been there. At some point, between our family systems, our socialization and our acculturation and our "schoolization", we start living a divided life where the body and the mind are separate. We live for the rest of our lives never healing that split. We observe the body as something to clothe and exercise, but not as an intimate part of who or what we are.

Part of our practice here is to turn inward and begin to heal the division between our body and mind. Our Western culture focuses on improving the life of the mind. Yet, here is an aspect of ourselves that we have to return to or reinhabit.

These are fundamentally somatic practices. I think when we get excited our energy always goes up in a constant effort of "trying to get out of our body". These practices work to bring our energy back down and inhabit our physical world. In my first years of practice I did not understand this. I thought it was ultimately not about transforming myself, but transcending myself. I don't know that transcending was easier, but with the "life of the mind" it felt natural to train myself to disembody. I had a lot of support culturally.

We have become a culture of users. So the earth doesn't participate with us, it's something we use and abuse. One of the wonders of the Buddha is that so much of his life is an archetypal story, which makes it a gift we can look at and learn from. He was born under a tree, he achieved enlightenment under a tree, gave his first teachings under a tree, and he died under a tree. This teaching about nature is incorporated into the story of his spiritual life.

I'm sorry to say, but Robert Bly wrote, "Buddhism's problem is that it's too cerebral." We know that it has that tendency. All religions, all things of the spirit, have the tendency to incorporate a transpersonal part into it. But that's not how this practice works. It's the way of the philosophy. Many of the early teachers were intellectuals and held Buddhism as a philosophy. But when I visit Thailand, I see a hierarchy there, a transpersonal piece. When you believe in spirits, you also believe in ghosts, so there is also a shadow side of that. But there is a very transcendent part, too.

Many of the practices we train in were not shared with the lay community until the 1940s. If you took robes, then you were exposed to the *Vipassana*, this insight practice. Otherwise, there was the *mantra* practice, this wonderful gift-giving culture of *dana*, and the fundamental precepts, which supported the *mantra,* with a spirit of devotion and faith. They didn't teach breathing techniques to the lay community. All of this was kept within the monastic community.

Then in Burma, Mahasi Sayadaw and Uba Kim starting taking it into the lay communities and began this evolutionary practice. One of the lovely things Uba Kim spoke of was "ringing the bell of the *Dharma*", which led to the teachings coming to the United States. Padmasambhava wrote about this many centuries ago: *When the iron bird flies in the sky, the Dharma will be carried to Land of the Red Man.* This has come true.

I remember our first retreat here in Jackson, Wyoming nineteen years ago with five retreatants. You didn't come here by accident. There are no accidents. You heard about the *Dhamma*, a process that would free you from your suffering. No matter how privileged, all human beings are included. In our own sensitivity, we suffer. In that suffering there is a longing for freedom. But there is a thread that you recognize, and then you follow that thread. All of you here are part of that thread and that thread reaches back over lifetimes.

You've been doing this for a while. It's too foreign to this culture. It's too new to this culture. I believe that everyone I meet has been doing this for lifetimes. Buddhism doesn't believe in reincarnation, we believe in rebirth. Rebirth means it just goes on and on. There is a continual thread that breaks and then reestablishes itself. Chogyam Trungpa was asked, "What is it that's reborn?" He simply answered, "All your bad habits."

This happens to be your good habit and somewhere along you touched this, who knows where and how. This is my belief. In some ways you are coming to reinhabit. You learned the practices of transcendence. That's what was done.

I think it was in 1991 the Dalai Lama met Western teachers at Dharamsala, India. Many people attended. One of the courses for the teachers was about disembodiment. The Dalai Lama was confused. "How can that be? How can Westerners feel disconnected from their bodies?" The Tibetan people don't experience this, and many Native peoples, the Mayan Highlanders, and the people in Thailand have a natural, cultural ease with themselves and their bodies. The Dalai Lama was totally confused, "How is it possible?" When he finally understood, he cried; because he realized this is a culture that has created a great internal split.

Many of you have heard stories of my growing up in El Salvador and Guatemala, a blond kid in the tropics. My nursemaid was a Mayan Highlander Indian, who taught me her language, which is a rather simple, sing-song language. The Mayan Highlanders are so gentle and sweet. There is something about them culturally, the split isn't there. My father had a cigarette factory in Guatemala for the Indians. He had been in Panama, Honduras, and other places for maybe fifteen years. Then there was a revolution and someone burned down my father's factory. I was with my nursemaid in the park when things blew apart in the town, with a lot of gunfire and violence.

My parents grabbed a suitcase and we flew up to Mexico City on an old DC-3, and then on to Lexington, Kentucky. I don't know what happened to me, but I suffered severe trauma, maybe from the gunfire. My mother was an intellectual and not terribly warm toward kids. Whatever I had experienced caused me to stop talking. My parents put me into a school for autistic children. After a year in that school I started speaking again. Then I was sent to boarding school in Switzerland, where I stayed through grade school and high school. Out of that experience I learned to dissociate. I think all of us learn this through different ways. But mine is an extreme story of it.

Years later, while still living in Lugano, Switzerland, I was almost eighteen years old and I wrecked a TR-4 by hitting a Porsche. Three months later I smashed up an MG-1100. I was destroying everything in my path. I was into complete destruction. I think that part of it was a cry for help. Another part of my acting out was the beginning of my trying to bring parts of myself together. Then, I spent time in Paris in the winter, cold and poor, disowned by my parents. Seeking answers, I moved to San Francisco in 1967, the Summer of Love.

I understood that I was looking for something, but I didn't know what. I tried psychedelics, which were a great blessing to me, but they also reinforced and supported my dissociation.

I read recently that in the United States, one of the wealthiest and most religious countries in the world, about 25% of us are part of the evangelical movement, which I see as seeking an answer "out there", outside ourselves. I too had this transcendent idea that I would be taken care of by something "out there". This reinforced the dissociative part of me.

I continued my seeking with an overland trek to India in the late 1960s. I didn't really understand what path I was pursuing or what the Tibetans were teaching. But I had learned to not to get into the body, but to get out of it, to live in the mind. It was really my transcendent ideal. When I first started these practices, I wanted to get high, and the concentrations would help me get out of here. For a long time I thought that was the way. I had good concentration and I was able to get out of my body.

But ultimately I came to two realizations: first, I was an escapist. I was a runner. I had left all my cultural connections with the West. I thought that if you burned all the bridges, you could be somebody else. When I came to these practices, I understood that even if I could settle my breath, there was so much still swirling around, I was still caught in my head. But, as I relaxed and things calmed down, the currents from my life also all settled down. Then came the second truth; like Singi, I was a split person.

One of my oldest friends, long before I went to India, had come from the University of Chicago, a psychologist named John Welwood. He was a really good friend. In the early 1970s he coined the phrase "spiritual bypass". I had become such a devoted "spiritual bypasser". It took a long time to address this realization, this does not happen overnight. There are layers. At first you need the transcendent parts. I think you need them so you'll have the strength to stay with this. So there the transcendent or transpersonal states are really helpful. But at some point, I had to return to the bridges that I imagined were burned. They weren't actually burned. Underneath it all was still the same old story. I was carrying the same trauma and the same baggage.

In the late 1960s, I was out there. For a while I could escape everything. But, then, I learned I had to turn around and start owning all this. In the deeper waters are these currents, and some are very old, either from childhood or perhaps another lifetime. Eventually, you have to confront the unresolved feelings. You realize that you must integrate all of you. It's not just about owning some high ideal or becoming some spiritually evolved person. It's about your whole being with its history of fragility and trauma. My trauma and difficulties in the end became my gift. I hadn't transcended them; I had only bypassed them for a while, now they were coming back.

I remember my first two retreats. There were six weeks of sitting and I didn't understand the instructions for the first ten days. I didn't listen. I had been constantly moving from boarding schools to all sorts of different places and my life felt very disjointed. For the first days I kept going back over my life trying to get a chronological order of the bridges themselves and what I had disowned, dissociated from.

From all appearances I was a happy guy, but I cried throughout my second ten days there. I hadn't cried since I was a little kid in Switzerland in boarding school. I had shut that part down and told myself, "You're going to be a tough guy." I wasn't, but I was pretending. Suddenly I just cried. I had disowned my suffering, but my suffering became my path back to wholeness. I had to drop into my body and realize that it held not only my history - this is one of the marvels - my body also held all of humanity's history. Your body, your genetic code, holds all of the history. You have to find a way to own it! You can't dissociate from it! You have to inhabit it!

I remember when I first came to this practice in my early twenties in Asia, I really wanted to get enlightened. For a while, I thought I could fast myself out of suffering. I just didn't want to be a screwed up teenager again. I knew that somehow, I had this instinct that I didn't want to do this again.

We have all suffered. We have all had this split. I think our culture has trained us to not be in our bodies. But even more telling, splitting off has damaged our sense of self-worth. I don't see that damage in Eastern cultures. It's unique to ours. It means that we don't actually believe in ourselves. There is this piece of self-doubt that has to be healed, if we are to be whole.

Even in athletics, which we think is about embodiment, I have come to realize there is also a transcendent practice when you reach a certain level. Embodiment has two pieces, it's about extremes. Sports can evoke great pleasure, as can sex or food or even a flower. It's just the sense of a body experience. The opposite is that constant discomfort, sometimes quite sharp, that we want to avoid. We try to keep the uncomfortable away.

This practice is not about either extreme. They refer to it as The Middle Way. The Middle Way is the subtlety where there is neither an extreme of discomfort nor the extreme of pleasure or excitement. There is this middle place, and that middle place is essentially what we are here to train in.

I'm not even a spiritual person. I think that's a fantasy. I don't care about that anymore. What I care about is: "Can I be true, can I be whole?" If I'm that, there is something marvelous in these teachings. It's possibly not transcendence. It's actually not something I get, it's something that I always was, actually what I have inherited. You can use lofty words like "Buddha Nature" and stuff like that. I think that can be helpful and a good explanation. It's also true that there is nobody to be, nothing to possess, no experience to have, and nowhere to go. *Karmically*, you are already happening. We are very complicated *karmic* creatures.

If you can learn to sit back and get that this is just about wholeness! The wholeness is the capacity of not shrinking from things, but, counter-intuitively, to open instead of close. That to me is one of the grandest parts of all this, to train oneself in the minutia, train oneself to own the body and the feelings and the mind. You're going to keep coming up against contraction. Our culture is based on stress. To counter that, we use protectionism, fear, circle the wagons, hide, defend, or we can actually turn it around and ask, "What have I learned? I have learned when contraction and stress inevitably comes, I don't need to get small. I can expand and own more of it."

We think we can solve things with our minds. I'm not saying there aren't certain things for which our thinking minds are useful. But from the Buddhist point of view, there is this middle way and I'll use the word "wholeness". The mind inhabits the body and is aware of it and owns it. There is an embodiment that has a phenomenal factor to it. When you're inhabiting your body with your mind you have intuitive wisdom. This wisdom is no longer about the faculty of thinking and analyzing and classifying and organizing, it's actually an intuitive knowing that comes from a whole body experience. I am not saying the mind isn't there. The mind is there, but part of its function is being used to inhabit, it's actually training itself to stay in the present moment.

As I have said many times, "You can't be in your body and be in the past or the future or lost in thought." You can squeeze in a little bit of thought. Ultimately, your experience and your wholeness is a mind that's connected and lined-up with a body that recognizes first its heart and then its freedom. This is another component of wholeness. Then to have the capacity for awareness itself.

Awareness can't be noticed anywhere else. It can't be in your thoughts. You are not following some sensation out the window or door. You have to be fully present and present in the sense of wholeness, a wholeness that recognizes its ultimate experience. There is this recognition. This is not about some big "AHA". It's simply seeing something that has always been there. It has no past or future. It's not based in time. But it's completely "experienceable", and seeable, knowable, and recognizable. It isn't dependent on the thunder gods or the people in the room or sense experience. It's something that has always been with you. There is a great comfort in its recognition.

But again, it's not something you hold or keep.

You get it for a moment, and then you forget when some thought comes along and your mind grabs that. It can only be recognized in a moment. It's not a stable thing, but it's recognizable.

You have to learn to stay in your seat. Your physicality is a gift that you have for a certain amount of time and it always carries this. When we can sit and not get lost in the complexity of all the sights and sounds and memories and plans, all the relative goings-on, then the recognition comes. But you have to have studied and know the relative experiences and know how they work.

You recognize that our senses bring temporary happiness, but they also bring temporary suffering. But there is something holding everything, including these relative experiences. There is a pure awareness. In Buddhism it has many names, but I don't want to name it or codify it or make it a thing. I think that's the danger. It can't be made into a thing, it can only be recognized. As it's recognized, it frees up the relative world so that we aren't bamboozled by our multifaceted world and its wonder. It's not just science; it's multifaceted and has great mystery involved in it. The physical world is also a transpersonal world. Our job is to hold all of it and see that there is something more. It's not to turn away from it, but simply not to get lost in it.

There is an actual healing that happens when we recognize the split and realize that the ideal of perfectionism and "never-enoughness" is the consequence of the relative world. We fell hook-line-and-sinker for that split. We have come to these practices to take the hook out and to begin to heal. The Buddha told us, "Within this fathom-long body is found all the teachings, is found suffering, the cause of suffering, the end of suffering, and the path to the end of suffering."

You are walking around with thousands of years of intelligence. What I have found is that the Western paradigm has been the life of the mind. What I have seen through Buddhism and psychotherapy and the mindfulness movement is that we are turning that around. What is it that we are turning toward? Toward this genetic code, when the mind makes contact and inhabits the body, there is a mystical awareness.

We have the term *deja vu*, which I think is happening all the time. Things occur, but we have blinders on and we miss them. But we are awakening to seeing a little bit into the mystical, the complex world that's not obvious. It takes some training. Sometimes I say we have on blinders because of our dualistic sense of self. If you can remove the blinders just a little, you can see into the collective consciousness that's happening around us and in us. I think the whole environment holds this consciousness and is a reminder of the power of these little creatures (ourselves) bound by history. Maybe you'll be around for a hundred years, but in time that's nothing. It's just nothing, not a drop in a pail of water.

I always like to read this poem by Hakuin Ekaku from the *Song of Zazen*.

All beings are of the nature of Buddha, as ice by nature is water.
How sad people ignore the near in search for Truth afar, like someone in the midst of water crying out for thirst.
Truly, is anything missing?
Nirvana is right here before our eyes, this very place, this pure lotus land, this very body, the Buddha.

Eduardo Galeano, the Uruguayan writer, reminds us, "The church says: the body is a sin. Science says: the body is a machine. Advertising says: the body is a business. The body says: I'm a fiesta."

I think that's enough tonight. I could babble on, but the truth is I've laid it out and in your own experience you are still healing from the busyness and the complexity, sometimes self-imposed, sometimes from the external world. You just need to sleep and heal and rest.

My job is simply to make sure you stay present here. I can encourage you to not remain limited by the relative world or your inability to stay with your breath or how many times you forget and go off and plan and tell stories and rehash memories. That's part of what happens here. I like what Chogyam Trungpa said, "We come to this and our job somehow is to wear the soles off the shoes." You have enough time to wear away the stories.

Coming together like this, the community has a wisdom factor that helps unhook little pieces of the story. One more traditional story, then I'll read a poem to close.

There was a child made out of salt, who very much wanted to know where he came from. So he set out on a long journey and traveled to many, many lands in pursuit of this understanding. Finally, he came to the shore of the great ocean.

"How marvelous," he cried and stuck a foot into the water.

The ocean beckoned him in further saying, "If you wish to know who you are, do not be afraid."

The salt child walked further and further into the water, dissolving with each step. At the end he exclaimed, "Now, I know who I am."

I like that.

Ram Dass said, "We are all walking each other home." I love that.

A poem to end here; it's called "The Rim of Time":

Sitting on the rim of time,
waiting for the breath,
some foothold on the mountain side,
some place to take a stand,
over and over disappointed,
until that that grasps floats, floats on the eddy of time,
saying, "This is my body found, a river carrying everything
and nothing."

CHAPTER THREE

FIVE HINDRANCES AND FIVE SPIRITUAL FACULTIES

There are two parts that I would like to work with tonight. The first is the five difficulties or Hindrances:

- Sensory Desire (*Kamacchanda*),
- Ill Will (*Vyapada*),
- Sloth and Torpor (*Thina* and *Middha*),
- Restlessness and Worry (*Uddhacca* and *Kukkucca*),
- Doubt (*Vicikiccha*).

Then I would like to move into the Five Spiritual Faculties:

- Faith (*Saddha*),
- Energy (*Viriya*),
- Mindfulness (*Sati*),
- Concentration (*Samadhi*),
- Wisdom (*Panna*).

These two balance each other. When there is enough concentration or collectiveness the hindrances actually move out. So at a retreat sometimes they don't bother you. But, what is also true, they can provide insight into our own process and operating system, particularly out in the vast world that we inhabit. These can all be dealt with using one single thing: mindfulness. Or, you could say awareness itself has the wherewithal to disempower them.

The Five Hindrances

A lot of the time awareness isn't there; and when it's not there, these hindrances become quite powerful. They can hold us in trance for a time.

Sensory Desire (*Kamacchanda*)

The first hindrance is wanting or desire. Again I say there is a healthy side to wanting, for example the desire to awaken. This is a positive and necessary recognition on the path. Also, the desire to help others is positive. But I want to speak about this as a sense experience.

In a way, we are simple creatures who seem to have one particular function, to hold or create as much pleasure as possible. That is the ideal. But by its nature, pleasure is part of the phenomenal world where nothing stays the same. So we may desire pleasantness and the Buddha said nothing about the pleasantness itself. Pleasantness isn't the problem. The desire is the problem. Instead of being with what's happening, we lean away from the present moment toward the future and the object of our desire. Whether it's lust, whether it's food, whether it's time, so much of our world is held by this.

From the fundamental practices point of view, I think there is an extreme in the Theravadan perspective that all sensual pleasure ends in suffering. That's an extreme and I don't know if I necessarily buy that as the whole story.

There is the capacity, and this is part of The Five Spiritual Faculties, and also of the tantric view of the spiritual experience, which is a heightening of seeing, smelling, hearing, tasting, and physical sensations to a little higher octave, so that we can actually see pleasure's nature more clearly. It, too, has this simple truth, even at the very high level, it changes. It's not a solid thing.

We are going to work with this. As householders, you have to have the wherewithal and wisdom to deal with sensual pleasure. You don't need a monastic practice renouncing all sensual experience. When it comes to pleasant sensations, we have an entire advertising industry telling us to participate in whatever pleasure they have manufactured for us. Buy it, get it, have it! And they are very good at persuasion. That is one side of the coin and all based on pleasant.

Ill Will (*Vyapada*)

The other side of wanting is aversion. I hope you don't experience this, but I bet you do. When something arises that is either not part of your view, is disparaging, makes you feel less than, or when someone hurts your feelings, your reaction is immediately to contract and defend your position. You want to avoid the unpleasant experience. We have a whole culture that is extremely critical, judgmental and righteous. Just as we have the experience of leaning away from the present by trying to capture or hold onto some pleasant feeling or desirable object, we also lean away to avoid unpleasantness by contracting, attacking, freezing, or running away. It's pretty simple.

As I said before, peace comes from accepting the impermanence of both the pleasant and the unpleasant. When we become defensive, we separate out and create a stronger sense of self.

We are also confronted with continual bad news that creates fear, which leads us to self-righteousness, isolation, and separate identity.

This causes us so many, many problems. The sooner we see that by its nature unpleasantness arises and passes away, and we don't get caught up in it, the easier we can be with it. It's just impermanent phenomena.

When the contraction comes, if you can soften and find forgiveness, a sense of gratitude, and ultimately a loving feeling, that sense of isolation and contractedness will dissipate and gradually fade away. We are going to work with these. They're part of the world we live in.

Sloth and Torpor (*Thina* and *Middha*)

We can have trouble recognizing torpor if we don't have enough energy to overcome the feeling of heaviness and dullness. You simply drift off, which isn't supporting this practice. We fade away from it. I know for myself when that happens, especially in retreat situations, it actually brings up my self-judgment or anger. "I paid my money, so I'm supposed to stay awake and get something out of this. Here I am just kind of dull." I'm quite judgmental about it.

Now that you've been here a little while, you're probably no longer as sleepy. When your life is difficult and you feel overwhelmed either in relationships or business or whatever, one of the natural reactions is to shut the system down, to pull the energy out of it. Then, that dullness and heaviness become a hindrance.

Sometimes it takes investigation. Looking into the storylines can be helpful. Other times, this takes mental energy and that mental energy has dissipated due to complexity or confusion. The practice is to deal with it. The investigation can go on, but we have to find ways to raise our energy.

Raising our energy may simply require us to take a few deep breaths. The Buddha suggested pinching your earlobes. If you know anything about acupuncture, it's interesting because there are a lot of energy points there. Open your eyes! Taking a brisk walk also raises energy. Physical activity brings oxygen into your system.

Restlessness and Worry (*Uddhacca* and *Kukkucca*)

Another hindrance is restlessness and worry. It's incredibly bothersome. There isn't anything to do about restlessness. There is just the ability to endure. It, too, has a nature. It arises due to causes and conditions. It's there for a time and it passes away. It's quite uncomfortable, because the mind cannot settle on anything. The whole body is moving, and it's very difficult to settle it.

We say restlessness is about the past and worry is about the future. A lot of times it's just a string of words in the mind that is trying to solidify or to make safe something in the future. That is all that's occurring.

From a practice point of view, first use mindfulness to see how it works and how it holds you captive! Then recognize that it's simply a string of words based on something in the future and not about the here and now!

Doubt (*Vicikiccha*)

The last difficulty has to do with doubt, self-doubt. I often describe this as a cork that keeps popping to the surface. It doesn't allow you to investigate, to relax, to feel okay, or to feel safe.

There is a voice saying, "This is too hard. I can't do this." Or, "I'm never going to get anywhere." It's self-disparaging.

Doubt can also lead you to question your path and the teachings you're hearing.

The Five Spiritual Faculties

I'm going to leave the hindrances and move on to the Five Spiritual Faculties, which will address the doubt and the other hindrances as well.

The Buddha described these Five Spiritual Faculties as five horses pulling a cart. The cart is *samsara*, the conditioned or habitual cyclical existence.

- The lead horse is Mindfulness.
- The next two horses, yoked together, are Faith and Wisdom.
- They are followed by Energy and Concentration.

These five horses pull us along toward the experience of release or *nibbana* or freedom. Mindfulness and the other faculties can balance any of the hindrances.

Mindfulness (*Sati*)

Mindfulness or awareness, if you notice, can never be in the past or the future. It simply arises in the moment. It's what "arises due to the knowing or the awareness itself". It's held as *sammapajanna*, which translates as "clear comprehension". Mindfulness influences the other four horses pulling the cart. It's only a momentary experience. If it happens moment after moment, and if we have a continuity of those moments, then clear comprehension or intelligence follows.

These aspects of the different horses are ways to clarify or classify our experience.

The first of these horses, mindfulness, is leading and is the heart of this. There is an intelligence that actually follows.

Faith (*Saddha*) and Wisdom (*Panna*)

We have faith and wisdom as one pair. Faith isn't an easy thing to talk about in the Western culture. It gets somewhat confused. But in this context, faith is the necessary piece that has to do with the heart. The wisdom piece has to do with the mind. So we have these horses in parallel, you can say heart and mind or faith and wisdom.

These teams have to be in balance. Faith, when coupled with wisdom, has tremendous power. You could also translate the word faith as confidence. When you come to this practice, I hope you have confidence in the teachings, the teacher, and in your capacity to practice wholeheartedly.

To me faith is a big deal, at least for myself. But, I like the word confidence better. We begin to have confidence specifically in the teachings.

One of the great points of release in my life was when I realized how important faith was. Then I had confidence in the teachings, the teacher and the Path. These pieces give us the power to release, so that we can see into how our experience occurs.

There has been some criticism of this word "faith". Yet, the power of an open heart, a sense of devotion, a sense of surrender, is such a positive force that has the power to balance. I know for myself, I have focused more on the mind, but as years have gone by I've seen more and more how faith, devotion, a sense of humility, and a sense of wonder play an important part. These all come out of the heart. When faith is coupled with the discerning powers of the mind, then you have the strength of these combined horses as they pull the cart of our conditioned habits along.

But too much faith can get out of hand. The Buddha disparaged what he called "blind faith". Blind faith is when you surrender your wisdom for magical thinking. I think in the Western culture we understand the wisdom factor intellectually. The faith or confidence factor, not so much. It's something you have to work on. I trust the cultural decision-making that goes on in us. One of the complexities in our Western paradigm is that we make a lot of judgments based on mind. You'll see that many Buddhist books, especially the ones translated in the past, keep referring to mind. A lot of intellectuals are drawn to Buddhism. Referring to this as "mind" distorts what it's really about. To me it's a misinterpretation of the original texts. The word "*citta*" really means mind-heart. The heart was always a piece of mind.

In the *suttas*, the Buddha describes a giant who is super strong, but he can't see well. He has a small friend, who's crippled, but sees very well. The giant, the power of faith, and the small guy, who represents clarity, come together with the cripple on the shoulders of the giant. Then, they can move mountains. Faith and wisdom together can accomplish great things.

Energy (*Viriya*) and Concentration (*Samadhi*)

The other two horses are mental energy and concentration. We are really good at mental energy, but not so much with concentration. This mental energy has to be steadied, so that it can be used by this cart of *samsaric* conditions as it moves toward awakening.

One of the difficulties with the mental energy goes back to the hindrances. Mental energy can become restless. That is its tie-in. The same with concentration, when there isn't enough curiosity or mental energy, then dullness comes and concentration becomes a hindrance and is no longer a supporting factor.

I want to clarify the difference between the energy of heaviness and dullness. That is energy of the body. The energy of these two horses is actually the energy of the mind. I see as I get older that I don't have the same physical energy that I once had, but I have as much mental energy as I ever had. In that way, you have to make a distinction.

The horse in this analogy is the mental energy. In some ways, it has to be inspired. It's inspired through faith, through the heart, which gives it the quality of curiosity of investigation that is necessary to support this cart of *samsara* on its journey toward awakening.

Like faith, when mental energy is out of balance, it can get lost and mushier and confused. In the years of my teachings, there are people whose inquisitiveness is so great, but they are wracked by suffering. This is actually a very positive thing, except it doesn't have the second horse of concentration. It simply has the mental energy that is driving its inquiry. But it doesn't have the balance. The cart will not go without the balance. Just like with faith and wisdom or heart and the mind, you have mental energy with concentration or the collectiveness as a balancing factor. Too much mental energy and it can never focus on anything. It just keeps jumping from question to object, over and over again without ever really satisfying itself.

Coming to retreats, one of the principal gifts we receive, which is counter-cultural, is we quiet the body and bring some collectiveness. Whether you know it or not, you are incredibly concentrated right now. A lot is due to conditions, even if you're mumbling under your breath, you just sit here and sit here and walk and sit and think about a lot of things. Still, because of the environment, you collect yourself. That collectiveness balances the mental energy that has great curiosity and questioning of "Who am I? How did this all happen? Where is this all going?" The mental energy is balanced by the steadiness of the concentration.

Sometimes I think we have a totally distracted culture. We view life from the position of what we lack. Everything is based on the five-second byte. We come here to counter-balance that. This is part of letting go of the cart of *samsara*. We think our culture is incredibly concentrated and focused, but I actually don't believe that. What we are talking about is different from achievement through will, determination and focus. We are not focusing on a stationary single object, but learning to concentrate on a moving object. That is the basis for insight practice. It's the ability to stay present with moving objects, which has its own means to collect ourselves. It's not so much about absorption, but we are learning something more important to our daily lives, collecting ourselves on a moving object.

Any place in the body, the breath, any awareness in the body, any somatic piece, is always moving. We say, "Let's sit up straight and create some stillness!"

Why are we creating that stillness? It's because we normally generalize our experience.

This practice is saying, "No, we are going to be really specific. We are going to still the mind, to see into the movement that is happening." That is essentially what we're doing. We are quieting the mind and recognizing that what seems like one unified experience is something more. When we break it down, we see the thoughts are not the same as the sensations and the sensations are not the same as seeing or smelling or tasting. When consciousness makes contact, it may only pause for a moment before it moves to another object. That's all it's doing. That's why sometimes you can get discouraged with these practices. It's easier to take a single object and be absorbed into it. But, in this case, that doesn't translate to the wisdom part. We have to settle in and see that consciousness arises in every moment and is constantly moving from one place to another. It never stays long in any one place. We are learning to surf on the moving objects, the seeing, the smelling, the tasting, the thinking, the planning, the remembering, the body sensations, etc.

You are going to be working with lining these things up.

Again, the lead horse, mindfulness (*Sati*) or awareness, is something that we forget. This is also a remembering process. But the awareness is always there on some level. If you look at your experience, you'll notice that you're always noticing. You can never get rid of it. It's always with you. We're trying to find ways to support the noticing, for our purpose of easing the burden of the cart of *samsara* that we are dragging along, this wheel of dependent origination that, through ignorance, is constantly recreating itself over and over. This is the whole principle we are working with here, suffering and the end of suffering as represented by this cart of *samsara*, the conditioned and habitual cycle of existence.

This is the building that we do. When you understand the potential of these Five Spiritual Faculties, then they turn into the Five Powers.

The Five Powers come when all these forces are balanced. In that balance, they can create a moment of release. This moment of release breaks our identity with the cart of *samsara*. And, it's only for a moment. But in that moment, one completely gets the *Dhamma*. Some say that is the beginning of the Path. That little break, which is that moment between things, one understands the *Dhamma* and one has complete confidence in the path itself. They call it *sotapanna* (stream-enterer). You enter the stream of *Dhamma* at that point. So you have complete confidence in the quality of investigation and this path that the Buddha laid down as *Dhamma*. You also have one hundred percent confidence that the relative "who-you-are" isn't "who-you-are". That was part of the *samsaric* construction. Now you lose your identity in your cultural conditioning. You are no longer caught with being from this country, with those parents, with these ideals. You break the cultural conditioning. This is an important realization in this process. You are still caught with sensual desire. Right up until the moment before enlightenment, there is this ego-comparison that goes on. You can be quite enlightened and still be a real problem, because of that comparing mind which doesn't evolve until full enlightenment.

I want to go back to this moment of breaking our identification with the cart of *samsara*. It's such an important thing in our experience. I've used this analogy before, but it illustrates my point well. There is a pendulum that swings back and forth, all the time. On one side is one to ten. That is the pleasant sensation. All human beings work so hard to keep the pendulum up toward the ten. On the other side is also one to ten, and that is the negative, the unpleasant. You do everything to avoid this side. There is a constant battle within everyone to win as much pleasantness as you can get and keep away as much unpleasantness as possible. That is the battle, and we use all of our intelligence, our energy, our creativity in this struggle.

The Buddha understood this. He also understood that because everything is changing constantly, the mind's awareness is jumping from seeing, to smelling, to tasting, to hearing, to body sensations, to thoughts, to memories, to plans, to whatever. It's just dancing. It's always in this dance passing a zero point. The zero point is really where it's at. But, because it doesn't have a charge, no one sees it. The practice here is to slow down the pendulum dance between the consciousness and the objects of experience, whether it's seeing, hearing, smelling, tasting, sensing, thinking, planning, forgetting, or whatever. It's always dancing. If we can slow it down enough, and if it's pointed out to you, you start looking at that zero point.

What is different with the zero point from the other points on the pendulum? In one, we used all of our energy to prevent unpleasantness, in the other where we used all our energy to maintain pleasantness. The Buddha called the zero point *nibbana*: "the blowing out of the war", this constant striving toward the pleasant and moving away from the unpleasant, this constant human battle. The Buddha also called this zero point simply "peace". This peace arises when we extinguish both the flame of desire for the pleasant and the aversion to the unpleasant.

You first must understand this on a conceptual level, then you see you always have choice. That is really what this is all about. You can choose to suffer, not to enjoy what you have, to want something else. You can also resist unpleasantness as much as possible. You will then stay on the wheel of *samsara*. Around and around you go. This little break is the point where you can get off. You see the process of the pendulum swinging and how you are caught. You understand your operating system and how you create and feel your suffering. Then you know how to release it. The next moment is the zero point and a moment of peace. We are trying to, first, understand where we are looking. Then by being really precise and clear where we are focusing we can realize that within this release is peace, if but only for a moment. We are no longer within this small box, this prison that we have created. There is no prison, because there is no you there. There is only peace. There is just zero point. There is no identification. There is no duality. There is just that. Doesn't that sound great? It's yours. That is what you're here for.

CHAPTER FOUR

FOUR FUNDAMENTALS:

CONCENTRATION, *VIPASSANA*, SINGLE TASTE, AND NON-DISTURBING AWARENESS

This is really about the world between the visible and the invisible. So much of this specific training is dealing with the physical world, that which is visible, that which is known to us. Ultimately, we are more interested in the invisible world. The Buddha, in his own experience of things, used the language of the super-mundane when he talked about *nibbana*. It was not something that could be classified or qualified in the relative language of the world. It was left as a mystery in the mundane world.

When I first went to India in the 1960s, I wanted to go to southern India and either rent or buy an elephant. I had heard that Arthur C. Clark, the science-fiction writer and author of *2001: A Space Odyssey*, lived in Sri Lanka. But, the monolith in his book was in southern India and there is a pilgrimage of circumambulation around it. I never made it to the monolith, but it did inspire me that there was something out there that was quite physical and, at the same time, very transpersonal.

At that time, I viewed Buddhism as very dry. I wanted the heart magic, not to spend my time looking at the bare facts. But the Buddha was just into the bare facts. He said we have a problem called suffering. He offered a diagnosis of the causes of suffering, which we know are attachment and grasping. His prognosis was "freedom", "*nibbana*", "liberation", something beyond the world of the senses and the known. He then gave a treatment, and the treatment was simply called the Eight-Fold Noble Path. You start with the basics, then go through the particular steps of understanding through the wisdom and ethics and practices. It's pretty simple stuff.

Tonight, I want to weave some of these parts together. We are in the process here of going through the treatment itself, since I think we all know about the diagnosis. We recognize the problem, and we also understand there is a possibility that given the right practice and the right environment, we can at least thin it out. I'm not saying we will eliminate suffering from our lives, but we can lessen its impact or, as I like to say, "Thin it out." I think it's easy for us to get into a slump in our practice. We drift here and there. But, it's simple. All you have to do is show up and watch your breath. It isn't anything spectacular.

I would like to work with the Four Fundamentals in a slightly different way. They come out of the Tibetan system, but they're kind of a map. The first part we simply name "concentration", or calm-abiding, or collecting, or *Samadhi*.

The second aspect is this word *Vipassana* or insight practice, which actually has many translations. But traditionally it means "to see". Sometimes *vi* is translated as "special seeing" or "seeing clearly". These days, I understand it as, "Seeing into the subtle." This is hard work. You have to discipline yourself to get here and get quiet. With this second piece, you begin to see into the operating system that you're dealing with, the emotions and the stories you tell yourself. You're supposed to be focusing on your breath, but I am just wondering, in the midst of all this, how much time today have you focused on your breath? It's just a question.

I like the term "calm abiding" as a translation of *vipassana*; but I prefer "seeing into the subtle". What is the subtle? It means we have to acknowledge our whole system and quiet it down.

Then we can see into the principal functioning parts of the psychology and that which is underneath everything.

The third piece I will just touch on is simply referred to as "single taste" or "non-dual" or "not this/not that". Actually, it's a kind of "oneness" that we can get to or we can experience or know something about. We understand that everything and everyone is part of a whole, nothing is separate.

The fourth aspect has to do with our daily lives. We are looking to see into the operating system and how it translates into the world that we know. I like the translation "non-disturbing awareness". Another translation that I like particularly is "ordinariness".

Concentration

These are the four things I would like to tease out a bit. These are the four fundamental principles. The first one is just the use of concentration, which is our ability to practice "one-pointedness". There is an exclusiveness in our deciding to bring our attention back to our breath, an exclusiveness based on concentration. We need some concentration, but not so much we go into a trance; although that in some ways can be very supportive and very helpful. But going into a trance does not help us with the second part, seeing clearly. Why do we sit? We sit to stop the body. Hopefully, then the mind will collect itself. I think that if we really understood the practice we would see it's very simple. In the Zen tradition, you keep your eyes open and you look at the blank wall. You just let the whole system settle down.

The Buddha was not interested in our psychology of the personal. He was interested in the principles that govern the human being and the human psyche. You can look at it as the analogy of the ocean. Our lives much of the time are just bobbing around on the surface of things. Sometimes we gain insight from an event or suffering that prompts us to see a little deeper. That is probably not the best way to achieve awareness.

This practice is, in a sense, a contrived way of settling the surface material. It's not that it isn't going to affect you. But the surface material isn't what we are ultimately interested in.

It's true that it will get purified just by sitting and observing the breath and not getting caught in your stories and your feelings about everything and what you make up about everything. If you can just sit with that, then what begins to happen - and this is why they call it "insight practice" - we begin to drop down beneath our surface material, below our likings and dislikings and preferences. As we drop down, we go from that surface material, which is very personal, to a connection that is more whole. It's a connection, not to our state or ourselves or separateness, but to a "less who you think you are" place. You start breaking down the separateness into "the universal", the "non-separateness". This is what the Buddha was interested in. Although the nature of the personal and the separateness is neither good nor bad, but as you can see, it includes all the components of suffering.

The Buddha's description is of the two arrows. The one arrow is for this body and all the complexities that happen *karmically*. Your life has only one destination: if you're lucky you get old, you get sick, and you die. This is everybody's story. That is the first arrow. No one has gotten out of this alive, yet. We have to come to that understanding.

But the second, the third, the fourth, the fifth, the sixth, the seventh arrows represent all the constructions that we make about the first arrow. We make up so much about our world. We walk around with our opinions and our views and create this perception of our world. Each of us is doing the same thing. We are walking around in these little bubbles of separateness. One arrow, and then we make up another one, then we make up another one, and we keep going. Our lives get very complex from this view point.

The Buddha taught that we can't change the first arrow. But the second and subsequent arrows, we can learn how to avoid those.

Vipassana

In that teaching he used the language of seeing into or insight into the complexities of our emotions and our mental story-telling and our mental manufacturing. Our job here is to see that clearly. It's not that you are going to sit here and not think. You're going to tell all kinds of stories. These are manufactured, but we believe they are the truth. As we calm down and begin to understand, we drop beneath the surface of our personal, psychological, emotional material to the universal principles that lie below. These principles are more than our individual stories. They are simply human nature or human truth. They are pretty simple.

One of the beauties of this practice, I think, is realizing the truth of *anicca*, impermanence.

Intellectually, you know everything is impermanent. But, ultimately, your brain doesn't believe that. Its nature is to try to solidify or concretize everything that it hears, it sees, it smells. It's always trying to freeze our sensory experiences in time so that the brain itself feels safe. That's what the brain is trying to do. But, that's not the whole truth. The truth is there's a constant buzz of flux of things arising and passing away at incredible speeds. One of the Buddha's simple truths was: If you really understand impermanence, you will know what happiness is. Why?

We are learning some very simple principles here. Number one, like a little kid, you have to learn how to let go of everything. We are primarily learning at a deep level how to let go. We think we all know; but, instinctually, because of the nature of our brains to concretize and freeze things and make up all kinds of views and opinions and judgments about everything, we actually create an illusion of separateness. We walk around in that separateness forgetting that this is just rolling along in a complete flux. There is nothing that we can hold on to.

I like the principle that the mind can create these views and opinions, and they appear solid. But, if you take a moment to check into the body, which is never in the past or the future, you can't put the same mind into the same body ever. There is always a river of information that is flowing. It's incredible. Genetically, there are millions of years of intelligence. So, we begin to realize that if we get really calm we can start to see into the flux of things, and we see then that we generate our own suffering through the concretizing and this mix of beliefs and emotions. We create tremendous suffering through our religions and our wars that go on. We're caught in it now.

The Buddha said we have to get below this stuff to understand what suffering is. There was a belief in the Buddha's time that there is an actual soul or a solid or some concretized thing that exists. But the deeper you go the more you begin to question the solidity, and you realize that impermanence, that *anicca*, is actually how things are. There is no solid thing here that you can actually grasp or call the Big Self or whatever. There is this sense of flux, but the illusion that we are able to freeze the idea of self-and-other. The deeper you go the more you began to understand. We walk around enchanted and in a trance of the world that we have created around us. But it's not the whole truth. It's only a piece of the truth.

So our practice is a deconstruction process. We are deconstructing what we constructed. The main construction is "who I think I am". As that concretization of who I think am begins to thin out, then there are moments of awareness. Actually there are many of these moments. But we are confused by thinking, "If I get enough of these pleasant moments, and if I can keep enough of the unpleasant ones away, then I'm going to be happy." So all we are doing is struggling between the pleasant and the unpleasant. The Buddha simply said, if you just stay in that struggle, you can't see what is apparent. What is apparent - they say someone has to point it out for you - is the Zero Point.

Single Taste

It's not any "thing". That's what is so deceptive about it. We are all built around the idea of a charge. That charge is either pleasant or unpleasant. We have a culture caught in this for an endless time. Waking up is recognizing this. As we begin to recognize it, that zero point, which has no charge, becomes enough. But how would you recognize it? You have to get really quiet. You have to sit there. You have to get quiet enough to hear what's deeper, underneath the subtle. Then that zero point, the Buddha used the word "*nibbana*", is not so fancy. Because it's not something. It's a zero point that exists and is actually all of these things and always in your experience. There are moments when you're not caught in this game of the pleasant or the unpleasant, and then the struggle between them and you stops. The Buddha called this "peace". This is a place of peace, of non-struggle. That is what actually happens, because once we start recognizing it, then the dualistic mind that is always making up self-and-other, this-and-that, begins to thin out. There is the "single taste". It's simply the possibility of this. The Pali translation of *atamayata* is "not there with the object". Suddenly you can release the known world. The release of the known world is a single thing. You could use the language of suchness or *is-ness*. It just "is". It's just "such". It's just "is".

With that suchness, you turn back to the material itself, the relative world. You don't do these practices to just disappear. You do them to find a way to live in this world, with it, but not of it.

This is a strange thing to say, but almost all emotions are in some way a distortion. It's not that you don't have them with this practice, but you're able to see them clearly and know them for what they are. Due to causes and conditions they arise, produce certain reactions that you've studied and you know.

The sitting practice is pretty simple. I have done years and years of practice in different systems. I have found two things that were so important to me over the years.

One was the capacity to keep my mind in my body. When there was a reaction, I could be on the frontline of recognizing "Oh, I'm angry" or "I'm sad." I could name it. I think for many years, I didn't understand emotions very well. I was a guy and I was taught to set my feelings aside. But I found out from this practice that emotions are a very important part of the life we live. They are not good or bad; but sometimes they fool us into speaking or reacting. So we can feel them in the body as they arise, and we can name them: "I'm anxious." I know when I feel anxious my mind makes up stories about controlling the world around me. Suddenly there is an incredible dissociative state. But if we can understand the process, "Oh, I can feel it. Oh, I'm anxious. Oh, wait, I'm afraid," then we have a choice. Immediately, just the knowing of it actually is part of the wisdom factor. Then we understand that we can choose not to react.

The other piece is this mind, the great story-teller. Sometimes I like to think of myself as sitting in a theater watching a movie called "My Life". I have never been inside an IMAX theater;

maybe I have spent too many years in India. I was leading a retreat in the Midwest last week and there was a huge IMAX theater and I thought, "Oh, my goodness." But, imagine we are sitting in a theater, and these story-tellers are telling these fabulous stories: What we think is right! What we think is wrong! How this all works! It's not that this is good or bad, it's my life on the screen. We have the ability to realize, "I'm just sitting in the seat, and the story, which is my identity, is playing." Then I have a choice. I can say, "Oh, that is just simply thinking, or it's fantasizing, or it's remembering, or it's planning." I know you don't do this stuff!

I always love Ayya Khema, the German nun. Her favorite term for this kind of mind activity was "nonsense". "Oh, my gosh! There I go again. Nonsense!"

Non-Disturbing Awareness

However, recognizing the content of what's happening is not necessarily the same as understanding the process itself. What we are trying to do is to differentiate between the content and the process. This is a process. We have to be careful because we get fooled by the content. But the ability to simply note what it is that's occurring is such a great relief, "Oh, it's thinking.

Oh, it's imagining. Oh, it's planning." But the ability to simply note what it is that's occurring is such a great relief. Then to recognize, "Oh, I can live my life in the complexity of it and know my thinking and know that I am not just my thoughts. I am actually much more than my thoughts. I am not just my emotional reactions, I am other than that." But we have to be able to catch our thoughts and reactions as we navigate a very complex world.

I like this phrase "non-disturbing awareness". You will have to teach yourself this. This is what is necessary to navigate, this non-disturbing awareness. You have to be able to see what is going on and to recognize it. Then you have a choice. Otherwise, we are just puppets controlled by past conditions and habit patterns.

This is why we sit here and study all this. We begin to understand it and see that we are so much more. Knowing that we are so much more is the awareness of non-separateness. We are one. We train our minds specifically so that we can drop them into our hearts. Our hearts actually know non-separateness. It's a lot of work to train your mind to not get lost in itself, and to give your mind permission to drop into your heart and to understand how things are. It's that simple. But it takes a lot of effort and training. It takes a lot of your time and resources. Ultimately, when we train the mind to drop into the heart, then it begins to recognize, "There is this non-disturbing awareness here right now simply knowing itself."

You've been walking around in it your whole life. You can't get rid of it. Just try to not be aware! You can get entranced, but that awareness is always there, always there. And, its nature is free. We have to go through these processes to actually get to this point.

"Oh, the awareness itself is just what it is. If I'm undisturbed, then the knowing that it is there is enough."

The nature of peace and non-separateness is available to you, as soon as you sort it out. That mountain has already been climbed. But again, it is about single pointed awareness. But we separate it into two parts, we create the stories. Don't get lost! You have every reason to continue.

CHAPTER FIVE

CARE, SPACIOUSNESS, AND EASE

This evening I want to explore care, spaciousness and ease. I think when we come to this practice there are some very simple principles that can be helpful.

Care

One of these is care. We can say, "Be careful."

Another important piece is caring primarily for ourselves. If you are not taking care of yourself, then your ability to stay mindful and to recognize the nature of *samsara* is limited.

It's also important to recognize the difference between self-care and indulgence. We are care-taking ourselves by coming here and renouncing the choices and the stimulus in our daily lives. We come to retreat and say, "I'm not doing that right now. I'm trying to live in a community where we are taking care of our lives." This is hard to do at home. Here, whether we are cooking, cleaning, or doing chores, we only have one or two jobs. The rest of the time you can spend taking care of yourself. To someone who isn't here, this may sound like an indulgence, but it's necessary.

I remember once I was teaching near Kansas City at a big Catholic church. There were maybe forty retreatants. Everything was all fairly normal until the walking meditation. At that point, three vans full of kids showed up with rap music blaring from their sound systems. Getting out of their vans and seeing people with their eyes down, not looking up and walking very slowly step-after-step, the kids were taken aback. To them the retreatants were weirdoes very emphatically walking back and forth very slowly. Watching the scene from the outside looked very different than from the inside.

Our culture has become a nation of sound-bytes and we all buy into it. But what you are doing here is basically very simple. You are just stopping. You're stopping. This is so undervalued in the culture that you have to come here for self-care. You have come to sit. You have come to still yourself and quiet down.

I always equate it with winds blowing across the surface of water (life), constantly creating waves that are stirring up the water. You come to a retreat and you put a series of pontoons around the whole area. The wind comes and the pontoons decrease the force of the waves. Our primary purpose here is to soften the winds of cultural change that are churning up the water. The harder the winds blow, the more difficult it is to see into the depths of what's happening. We come, put the pontoons out, and dampen the waves. After a couple of days, the anxiety we are carrying and the expectations we have of ourselves in the cultural complexity just collapse. That was all part of the surface, the waves. The stories and events and ideas are part of the surface material. We can release those quite quickly.

As we slowly begin to drop below the surface the water starts to get a little clearer. But there are currents whipping up the particles in the water. These currents are often based on the past, sometimes a long time ago and seemingly having nothing to do with the present. Often they are emotions that are incomplete from way, way back and they come as currents. The practice here is first to accept that they will come, capture you, and hold you for a while, but you understand they have the nature to come and fade away.

There are other currents that will come and hit, sometimes with a lot of sadness, or anger, or confusion. They, too, come and fade away.

You need time to do this practice. I am a great advocate of nine-day retreats at a minimum, because there are so many stages and so many strong currents that you are going to touch and release, touch and release. You think you are finished, when, damn, something from childhood comes. People can do therapy for years and think they have completed all that. Then, at a retreat, some old wound will pop-up again. This isn't about completion, it's about movement. And sometimes it's old movement. It's touching into incomplete feeling bases that are there, feelings that you can feel and touch, because this is your life.

As you go deeper you begin to see the particles are farther apart and the water is clearer. At that point you can actually touch whatever that word "faith" is. You begin to trust that this natural unfolding, this process, works. You're willing to hang in there with it. It's all about being here and caring for yourself, so that as you move deeper into the water and the particles are settling, you can see farther into the depths. This is all about your taking care of yourself to be here.

Again, there is the balancing between the openness based on the heart and the deep understanding based on the mind.

Spaciousness

When the particles are spread out we begin to recognize the openness and spaciousness. Suddenly we recognize the value of all the self-care needed to arrive at this place of spaciousness. You are no longer a condensed self. It's as if you begin to see and recognize more clearly, whether you're looking at a chipmunk or at a tree, everything in nature seems to be relevant to that awareness. "I've been so busy that I haven't looked closely."

Then we start seeing the spaciousness, because we no longer identify with who and how we think we are. This is part of moving into the deeper water.

It's interesting, we have created a prison for ourselves. Even though we don't realize it, we are walking around in boxes that we have created. Our fear and our desire actually confirm the strength of the walls.

When we poke holes in our prison walls, we begin to see outside ourselves into what is really true. There is phenomenal space that is unlimited. *We* put the limits on things. We, ourselves, have built the prison.

The practice, when it's properly held, begins to loosen our self-imposed bonds. We instinctively contract at the thought of something bigger. When we say, "I don't know," we contract. Here, we have gone deep enough that we are not afraid. "Maybe I can lose my limited senses and look at a tree, look at the sky, with an open heart." We are no longer limited to the self-referential.

It's actually experiential, an experience that is bigger than the language we have to express it. Language is such a limiting factor. Within the experience there is so much that happens, we are closer to the primal in those moments, even though it can't be identified or talked about. But there is a feeling of this vast, open space that allows the purity of the senses to be experienced, even before perception has reached the point of mental formation.

We are really trying to stay on this edge of pure perception, without manufacture. If we allow it to move to the pleasant-unpleasant, then we create identity with it. At a deeper level, we don't try to create identity, we simply loosen the walls of our duality and our ability to stay in pure perception and stay out of the mental formations.

Pure perception is being able to identify something, but not make-up anything about it. It's like, "Oh, that's there and it is what it is." This to me is where the unhinging of the cart of *samsara* begins to happen.

Ease

Just the wonder of recognizing that I'm not limited to what I think or who I am or my views and opinions about it – instead it's pure experience - then there is the possibility of relaxing into the wonderful state of ease.

When ease and spaciousness are there and non-identification is happening, then the hinge that is holding the cart of *samsara* gets really wobbly. Ease and spaciousness come through the senses and are recognizable. But the ease is feeling-based.

Suddenly, I'm not trying. I have surrendered to present experience and the heart says, "It's okay. I know you can't know what is going on. You've stepped into an enormous world that you can't know." You are not going to retract from that but venture into the "it's okay not to know".

If I can stay with "not-knowing" then the separation between me and everything else is broken down. Then unhinging happens. Unhinging would be terrifying, if it happened suddenly and to someone who had not been doing this work. But because we have gone through stages with our old stories and identification and history and suffering, we now are deep enough to lose a sense of where we started. We are no longer who we thought we were. Suddenly, what seemed somewhat solid is no longer solid.

Once we begin to recognize that we have unhinged a little, we are at ease with not knowing. There is a recognition that the mindfulness, as the lead horse, has not gone away. It hasn't disappeared. The awareness is there, but it's not the same awareness.

The awareness before was based on the duality of self and everything else. It was in the framework of the dualistic world, which the Buddhist teachings identify as "The Two Truths".

One truth is the relative world that we inhabit. In this practice we have to go through the relative world as the path to the absolute. The Buddha's teachings are about the relative way of moving through it.

But the other truth is the absolute. This other side you could call "The Big" because words don't amply communicate what I want to convey. It no longer has a need in itself. It's simply the something that you are born with, that you've been walking around in your whole life. It doesn't need the relative for its knowing. It's simply the awareness of the awareness itself, which isn't hinged by anything.

One of the truths of that awareness is that it frees everything up. So nothing can be held by it. In that way, I started to say "our ability", but ability throws it into a form and this isn't form, this is an expression of awakening or enlightenment. This is your natural birthright, sometimes called "Buddha-nature". But I don't really care what it's called, I want you to know that you already have this. It's not about your personality. It's not about your history. It's something that is inherent. It's a gift at birth. With enough wherewithal to the relative, we can begin to acknowledge it and realize that one of its fundamental truths is that it has the power to let go of everything. If it can let go of everything, then that which suffers doesn't have to be there.

In the description of the ocean that I shared earlier, I talked of the particles and the undercurrents that grab and hold us. In many of his universal teachings the Buddha stressed the importance of ultimate release. I want to go back to the analogy of the waves that come and stir up the waters and the pontoons. We only have the insight to see a couple of feet under the surface. It's so much about the relative life based on survival, on money, sex, and rock-and-roll, our attachment to things, or loss. This is about the first six inches of the sea of our experience. For some people that is good enough and they are content with that and they figure out ways to survive until they die.

Then there are those who, for whatever reason, are inspired to look deeper. I have this sense that as I go around teaching, this isn't the first time that you've come across this. From my experience, this has been going on for a long time. You have been the quintessential seeker, who has been through a lot. Sometimes you've found a little piece and sometimes not. But there has been that need to find and to seek. That in itself is a wonderful quality, at least at the beginning, and the seeking is necessary to allow you to see the nature of this first six inches of surface material.

You see that the new car or house or relationship isn't the end-all. There is this curiosity that begins the process of coming here and coming again, because the process is long. From my point of view, your journey has involved many lifetimes. We have been going through things countless times and the process is refining itself and us as we go along. In the first foot or two under the surface, there is a lot of seeking and testing and trying and hoping. But that experience deals with the material world and with time, and with desire, and with fear.

We come and we sit and the system begins to settle. As it settles, as you have found out, there are the currents that are below the surface and many times they come to awareness, sometimes from lifetimes of habits and *karmic* conditions, and they attach to us. They have a psychological need for us to see them and to become aware of what has entangled them.

When I first came to this practice, even though I had been around Buddhism for some years by then, I didn't understand the fundamental teachings. Perhaps someone born into it might have gotten it, but I didn't have that advantage. But I had a belief that somehow I could get out. If I got a little deeper, I would get out of all this.

I did a pretty good job. Many of you have practiced different spiritual traditions that released you from some of those currents and from the past. There was a transcendent quality that affirmed your spiritual path. But there also can be a tendency toward "spiritual bypass". If you hangout long enough in these traditions, you will have to turn your attention to the nature of these currents and old sticky stuff that you would like to bypass. I can say that I did a really good job of bypassing.

When I came back to the West, I couldn't understand anything about this culture. I had grown up in Europe and I really didn't know anything about anything. It was such a shock that I had to make a living; I had to get along in partnership. I was blind about everything in the sense of cultural complexity.

In a way, you have to work backwards on these patterns. If you had a really good childhood, everything would be cool. I've met monks who had such good moms, everything was great. But if you didn't have that, there is a lot of stuff to work out, especially the psychological relationship to power, money and sex. We have to use some of this spiritual seeking to deal with those issues. If you don't deal with your issues, you can go deeper, but you won't have clarity to untangle your tangles.

I remember going overland to India and ending up in jail a few times: first in Greece and then in Turkey. I got totally lost and incredibly sick in Afghanistan. You would think that somehow I would have cleaned it all up. But, unfortunately, I didn't exactly do that.

We'll keep working on this, because it's so much about the relative world, relationships, money, power, sex. I only try to present it, but you have to come at it from many angles to understand that it's "not this or that". It has a non-dual flavor.

Awakening isn't something you do; it's something you recognize, something that essentially is already yours. Because we are still dragging a cart, we have to keep the primary horse (mindfulness or memory) at the forefront, and train ourselves in remembering. That has to be balanced with the horses of steadiness, intelligence and heart. Then you are going to be fine.

CHAPTER SIX

THE ONE SEAT

I want to start with basic Truth. The Buddha taught for forty-some years, and it is said he taught the same thing over and over. He taught the Four Noble Truths. This is the fundamental foundation.

The First Noble Truth

Unfortunately, it begins with the truth that all born into this world are subject to pain, which results in suffering. Certainly, all of you have treaded the waters of suffering and realize that perhaps there's a path that leads out of it, away from it, or transforms it.

The Buddha was very clear. He said, first of all you have to understand suffering. To understand is to recognize suffering has a cause.

The Second Noble Truth

The Second Noble Truth he called *tanha*, which translates as "grasping" or "craving". The grasping has the consequence of suffering now and in the future. Grasping has obvious forms, but it has very subtle forms, too: liking or disliking whatever is happening, it's not enough, it has to be different and if it was different then it would be alright.

As we go on and on, we keep fighting in this war with *tanha* - this grasping - trying to achieve happiness. But grasping simply recreates itself over and over. There's an endless battle between good and bad, happy and sad, right and wrong.

These practices, as we understand the causes and the conditions behind them, are the path of release.

The Third Noble Truth

The Buddha said the Third Noble Truth is the truth of release. Letting go doesn't have to be everything at once. It can be in very small increments. There are little moments when we recognize the suffering, we realize that we are grasping or clinging or exaggerating or minimizing. We see it and know it for what it is. In this knowing, there's a moment where we can let go of the hook. That letting go is what the Buddha pointed at.

This ultimate release is what the Buddha called

nibbana or "the blowing out of the self and grasping".

The Fourth Noble Truth

His Eight-Fold Path was the Fourth Noble Truth. It's the way for us to see the causes of suffering and the components of the path to liberation. It's actually pretty simple.

Often the Eight-Fold Path is separated into three factors.

When we recognize the causes of suffering and we release them, we have insight into the Wisdom Factor. This primary factor includes Right Understanding and Right Intention.

The Wisdom Factor influences the second factor of Non-Harming Conduct. Do no harm! This includes Right Speech, Right Action and Right Livelihood.

Concentration is the third factor. It is our focus here.

You have already experienced suffering. I believe you are all intelligent and you have seen into the causes and have realized there's a path to liberation. You have designated this time to explore this path. Collecting ourselves, which we are doing here, gives us the opportunity to steady our bodies, our minds and our hearts. Then we can have insight into how things work.

With this Wisdom Factor we begin to untangle who or what we think we are. As we untangle, that part of us that meticulously created and clung to a separate identity begins to thin. As it thins, we come to recognize the suffering our clinging and belief in a separate self has caused.

What does that awareness of the suffering do? It opens our hearts. We have come full circle and returned to the Wisdom Factor, which releases the duality of self and other, sees the unity in all things, and presents the possibility of creating an open heart. That's the path. That's what we are up to. Over and over again, you will be experiencing, exploring, and learning about these Four Noble Truths. They are the bedrock of this understanding and practice.

Once we really have an understanding of the Four Noble Truths, we move on to explore the practice itself. The practice, in its fundamentals, is that this mindfulness is simply a somatic awareness. It's of the body. Sometimes I think, "Well, did you ask for this thing?"

We are born into a perfect vehicle for exploration, a vehicle that actually has all the foundations for awareness, and that vehicle is your body. This means you don't have to search somewhere else for the tools. They exist within your body. The fundamentals are "we have a mind, we have a body, and we have a heart". The mind must inhabit the body to know the heart.

So our most basic training is bringing full awareness to the function of the body itself.

I find interesting our present culture's fascination with mindfulness and the present moment. In the West, we are only now recognizing a truth that has been taught for thousands of years. I can't look at my body and where it is and what it inhabits and not say this is a "grand mystery". I see a tree or a creek or the Angus cows, the creatures of this world, even the insects, as part of the mystery. In Asia there are insects all over the place. Within ten yards, there are an incredible number of inhabitants.

There's this truth, being in the body is very pragmatic sense but there's also a sense of mystery. We could view our world from a scientific format or we could hold the science with the mystery. I sit more in the camp of holding both.

I have been doing this practice for fifty years, and I have inhabited a lot of worlds in that time. That's why I am completely convinced that this is a grand mystery. As the years have gone by, I have looked at and experienced a lot of traditions. I'm not an intellectual. I am pretty simpleminded in many ways. What I really needed was teachings that were simple. That's why I came to these insight practices, I didn't have to remember much. One of the beauties of all my years in Asia, all I needed to do was to sit down and shut up and turn my mind to observe what was happening inside.

Over my years of trying to find the proper lineage and teachings that would help me, I recognized something in the Venerable Ajahn Chah of Southeastern Thailand, Yasothon Province. He liked it simple. He came from a farming community.

There's a lineage in the north of Thailand from the 1850s. Ajahn Sao was the teacher of Ajahn Mun. This last winter I went to Ajahn Sao's monastery. But Ajahn Mun wasn't into monasteries. He was a simple Dhutanga monk, practicing the thirteen austerities.

These Thai monks have a big umbrella that's kind of a mosquito net. They carry it around with their begging bowl and their three robes and sometimes flip-flops and that's it. Ajahn Mun lived in Northern Thailand as a wanderer.

I so love the old yogis, the wanderers who war against institutional lives. Ajahn Mun was one of those. I love the fact that Ajahn Chah only met Ajahn Mun for three days and he became Ajahn Chah's root teacher.

Simply because of who he was, Ajahn Mun's sense of liberation was directly passed to Ajahn Chah, who then passed it to many others. In some sense we think of these great yogis as transcendent, especially the ones who were not in the monasteries. They were beyond ordinary beings in that way.

I have several things I want to read tonight and I'll start with this one from Ajahn Mun, which always touches me:

In your investigation of the world, never allow the mind to desert the body. Examine its nature, see the elements that comprise it, see the impermanence, the suffering, the selflessness of the body, while sitting, standing, walking or lying down. When its true nature is seen, fully and lucidly by the heart, the wonders of the world will become clear. In this way, the purity of the mind can shine forth timeless and delivered.

To me that's really a great teaching, because this practice is not an intellectual pursuit.

However, this is a discipline that trains the mind to inhabit the present. In the present is where freedom and liberation exist. There's no need to chase other things. This is enough. It's not easy, as you all can see. It takes a lot of focus to not get caught by your mind, by the past or the future. I know you all know this. But, it's my job to say, "Please, you don't have to get on that train of association. You can say, 'not now,' and come back and sit in the presence of this body, this vehicle for awakening this time around. Own it, recognize that it has the power and the wisdom and at the heart of it, it has liberation!"

We go from that to the words of the Venerable Ajahn Chah:

You will see when the heart/mind is unattached, it's abiding in its normal state. When it stirs from normal because of various thoughts and feelings, the process of thought construction takes place, in which solutions are created. Learn to see through the process. When the mind has stirred from the normal, it leads away from right practice to one of the extremes of indulgence or aversion and thereby creating more illusions, more thought construction. Good or bad only arise in your mind. If you keep a watch on your mind, study this one your whole life, I guarantee you'll never be bored.

I love the fact that he calls the "unattached heart/mind" state normal, even if it only lasts for moments. However, this does not mean there are no thoughts, which can be confusing.

We think that somehow we come to meditation practice and we're going to stop thinking and then everything will be alright. But that's not the way it works. It's simply not being bothered by the thoughts. So we sit with the sensations in the body. Sometimes there are reactions of liking and disliking. If they are strong, then there are emotions and reactions. There's a constant stream of thoughts, but in Buddhist psychology they are not considered any different than the sensations in the body.

Sensations in the body are always there, just as thoughts are always there and moving through. But we give the thoughts so much importance that somehow we don't take in the whole world. In a sense this rips us off. It doesn't allow us the fullness of the opportunity.

We only have a certain amount of time. I was wondering, "How many fewer breaths do you have left in your life than you had when I started this talk?" The recognition of that is the opportunity to ask, "How do I live in the fullness of the opportunity, without being caught in the future or the past, but actually inhabit this marvelous place, this marvelous time?"

So I am moving on to several other quotes from the Venerable Ajahn Chah. One way you can look at this practice is what he simply called the "One Seat", the practical fundamentals of how this works. I'll try to explain it, and then I'll read his material around it.

As a human being, you have five senses, and your mind. In Buddhism, your mind is considered a sixth sense. One of the descriptions from the Tibetan Wheel of Life is of a house. This house has a door and five windows, representing the mind and the five senses.

The practice is to put a chair in the center of the room. The chair is your knowing, your presence, and your awareness in the center of the room. Then open the door and all the windows and see what happens. This is Ajahn Chah's description:

Just go into the room, put one chair in the center, take the seat in the center of the room, open the door and windows and see who comes to visit! You'll witness all kinds of scenes and actors, all kinds of temptations and stories, everything imaginable. You're only job is to stay in your seat. You'll see that it will all arise and pass. Out of this, wisdom and understanding will come.

I'd like to give you another quote by Ajahn Chah that I believe is at the heart of it.

The visitors to your chair consist of images, plans, memories, dreams, thoughts, emotions and many others. Once you acknowledge their presence, they will be happy to leave. However, you have to be sure to notice them and not let them take over the conversation going on in your mind. How will you sit silently with these visitors? Do you watch them come and go, or do you try to entertain them?

Here is another quote from Ajahn Chah. He also said:

I'm telling you it's great fun to observe closely how the mind works. I see the mind as merely a single point.

Do you see that this place is where the chair is? I'm going to give you some more. Ajahn Chah continues:

Mental states are like guests who come to visit this spot. Sometimes this person comes to call; sometimes that person pays a visit. They come to the visitors' center. Train the mind to watch and know them all, with this alert awareness. This is how you care for your heart and your mind. This is the Buddha's firm and unshakeable awareness that watches over and protects the mind. You're sitting right here since the moment you emerged from the womb. Every visitor that ever has come to call has arrived right here. No matter how often they come, they always come to the same spot, right here. Knowing them all, the Buddha's awareness sits firm and unshakeable.

Simply know who the guests are as they arrive. Once they have dropped by, they will find that there's only one chair and as long as you are occupying it, they will have nowhere to sit. The next time they come there will also be no chair free. No matter how many times these chattering visitors show up, they always meet the same person, sitting in the same spot. There's only one seat and you're sitting in it. How long do you think they will continue to put up with this situation? Everything and everyone you have ever known since you have experience the world will come to visit. Simply observing and being aware, right here, is enough to see the entirety of the Dharma.

This one has a repeat of the beginning, but the end is what is important. Hear these words from Ajahn Chah.

As I see it, the mind is like a single point, the center of the universe, and mental states are like visitors who come and stay at this point for a short or a long time. Get to know them well and become familiar with the pictures they paint, the alluring stories they tell you to entice you to follow them. But do not give up your seat; it's the only chair around. If you continue to occupy it unceasingly, greeting each guest as it comes, firmly establishing yourself in awareness, transforming the mind into the one who knows...

You can see, the two quotes are similar but the second one ends with new ideas. And Ajahn Chah continues:

... the one who is awake, the visitors will eventually stop coming back. If you give them real attention, how many times can these visitors

return? Speak with them here and you will know every one of them well. Then your mind will at last be at peace.

These are simple instructions. That's what I like about them. As you sit here, you are the center of the universe. With these doors and windows as the senses, there's a knowing sitting in the center. What happens? A beautiful sound comes flying through that sense window to that center. Your job is not to deny it or move away from it. It's simply to say, "Welcome, please come in." And they will come. Sometimes more than one will come.

I think when you are sitting there, suddenly there's a barrage of clowns and jugglers and they carry little signs "vote for me". All sorts of things come in and try to entice you to leave your seat.

How many times have thoughts of the past or plans for the future come in and pull you out the door? And you went away. I think of it as the little choo-choo train and you get on and away you go. You are still sitting in your seat, but you suddenly wake up and realize, "Oh my goodness, where have I been?" What's nice is that if you were on a real train, you would have to get on another train to come back. But with this imaginary train, instantaneously, you can come back to your seat.

Awareness runs this, you know. It's true you will keep getting entrapped by this over and over. It's really fascinating. You will get enchanted, you will get entranced. But the practice is: with awareness you begin to recognize that thoughts and sensations appear and disappear. They are not permanent. The only power they have is the power you give them. While they seem so enticing, they are really not anything. Yet, they seem to be so compelling and entrancing that we will follow them anywhere thinking, "If I follow that thought, it will create the circumstances for happiness or for avoiding unhappiness." One of the words I love is "bamboozled". It's true, we get bamboozled.

You are sitting there in your body and the body and the senses and the mind are the house. There is this knowing in the center that you inhabit and its presence has a phenomenal awareness. That knowing, that awareness itself, is incredibly unique. Everything that comes through the windows and the door is part of an ever-changing world. It's part of impermanent phenomena that has no value or solidity. That's where we live most of the time. But, now, sitting in this chair, with this knowing, there's more to it. There's the consciousness that touches each of these sense doors and it arises and passes away in its relative nature.

But there's something about the seat and it's why I became so interested in this somewhat esoteric teaching. This teaching was ridiculed and not taught by the hierarchy of the Thai and Burmese traditions until the latter part of the past century, because it didn't follow the *Abhidharma* completely.

This last winter I went to a remarkable temple in the center of Chiang-Mai. There's a university and a big *cheti* (*stupa*) surrounded by the ancient center of the old city. There are two temples and space for thousands of people to circumambulate around it. It's gorgeous. One of the temples is to Ajahn Mun. Inside they have made a replica of this skinny little monk sitting cross-legged in a meditative posture. I don't know if it's made of rubber or plastic, but it looks life-like and real. I took pictures. He looks so regal you could almost see a smile on his face, as if he were thinking, "You guys are caught, stop it. Get over it!"

I was so touched I stayed awhile and I went back again simply to sit. The Thai people come in and do their prostrations and bring flowers and money and other gifts. There's a great sense of devotion.

Next door is another temple dedicated to Ajahn Maha Bua's, who like Ajahn Chah, was

Ajahn Mun's disciple. Ajahn Mun wrote one poem at the end of his life, when he was housed in a monastery in Bangkok. The poem is twenty-five pages long, and it's all about releasing the aggregates, these components of mind and body, form and consciousness. But this poem is from Ajahn Maha Bua and this is the place I want to go:

Whatever arises has to vanish. Whatever is true, whatever is of a natural principle, in and of itself, won't vanish. In other words, the pure mind won't vanish. Everything of every sort may vanish, but that which knows the vanishing doesn't vanish. There with the knower does not vanish. This vanishing, that vanishing, but the one which knows they are vanishing doesn't vanish. Whether or not we try to leave it untouched, it keeps on knowing.

This is really an important piece. Ultimately, we begin to recognize that we inhabit that chair in the center and that the relative part of us is constantly tripped up by the sense-doors and thoughts and memories and images, and also that we believe that our happiness and our freedom are dependent upon those things. We are being bamboozled. If you believe that happiness stays no matter what, and we are talking about a world that's in constant flux and change, you're being bamboozled. It's not possible that happiness is constant in an ever-changing world. We begin by saying, "Okay, I won't be fooled, I will keep my seat, and I won't keep running out the windows and doors, no matter what comes and presents itself."

Sometimes, I think of it inside myself. I just sit there, things come, and I bow to them. I love bowing. I think it's such a profound and humbling practice. Sometimes it's very enticing stuff. Yet, you have the power to bow to it, to honor it, without rejecting it saying, "I don't like you. You're bad. Get out!"

You simply let it come, be known, and go through. We can do that and simply observe this stuff going through. We also see there's something that's not going through. This is what Ajahn Maha Bua was talking about, there's something that doesn't change. Ajahn Chah would call it "pure awareness".

This is your birthright. You have always had this and it's not affected by how many times you screw up, by the way. It can never be damaged. Its nature is completely pure and it's not dependent on anything.

Part of our practice is to learn to stay in the seat and to recognize that our ability to let go is based on that pure awareness itself. This is saying, "I'm free and I let things go." This is really pure awareness. I hope this is helpful to you. Pure Awareness is not dependent upon meditation either. It's something that just exists, but, you have to learn this in stages.

I wish I could just touch your head with a peacock feather and magically you would understand. Sorry!

CHAPTER SEVEN

THREE CHARACTERISTICS AND THREE SUBTLE CHARACTERISTICS

As we settle, we begin to touch on what the Buddha was actually interested in. A lot of what we confront is psychological, a lot is historical, and a lot is cultural conditioning. But he wasn't so interested in that. He wanted to see how deep we can go.

These deeper levels have universal qualities. They are no longer about the individual or the personal. They are simply qualities of being.

They are so fundamental, but yet they have to be emphasized over and over. Traditionally, we call them the Three Characteristics.

Tonight I am going through the Three Characteristics and then I will move on to the more subtle characteristics that are even deeper.

You have to go through the Three Characteristics over and over again. I always thought, "Well, maybe, if we could truly understand these then our search would be over." Actually, it's about the clarity of being able to move through the world, from the very depth to the surface, while keeping a sense of clarity and openness and spaciousness and kindness.

The three most fundamental characteristics are called (in English and in the Pali language):

- Impermanence (*Anicca*),
- Suffering (*Dukkha*),
- No-Self (*Anatta*).

Those are the Characteristics, which you have to go through over and over again. And the deeper ones are the Subtle Characteristics. They are:

- Simply Emptiness (*Sunnata*),
- The Is-ness of Things (*Tathata*),
- Not-There with the Object (*Atamayata*).

Impermanence (*Anicca*)

The truth is that we all know impermanence. That is a given! We have intellectual recognition or understanding, but we actually don't know it.

That becomes the trick here, because it takes a certain collectiveness and wherewithal to have each different level of insight into the nature of impermanence. It's so basic. It's so fundamental.

It's the bedrock of Buddha's teachings. It's an obvious, but not understood, truth.

Part of the practice is to see that we are pretty simple creatures. The Buddha set it up in a rather simplistic way. He looked at it as the aggregates or the components that make up who we are. It's not complicated, but as we investigate we see that it's actually quite deep.

He said there were five aggregates.

The first is form, we walk around in form in these bodies.

Then there is feeling: pleasant, unpleasant and neutral.

With feeling comes perception or recognition of the objects, which is connected to memory. Perception doesn't do anything with the object, it's simply a purity of perception. It recognizes something, but doesn't do anything with it.

Under that are the mental formations, which have to do with feelings, they have to do with imagination, and with all kinds of constructions. There is the purity of the recognition and then there is the messing with it. This is what we are famous for.

These are all relative states.

The fifth aggregate is simply consciousness. Consciousness arises and passes away. It happens at tremendous speeds. Consciousness is always in relationship. If it's not there, you're dead. That's a pretty easy one to recognize.

Because of its nature, when consciousness rises, it touches one of the four other aggregates. It may be in the body, it may be a feeling tone, then a recognition or memory, then the messing with it.

Consciousness is in this phenomenal dance that focuses on an object briefly then moves on to somewhere else. We have the illusion that this dance all happens at the same time. But, if we look closer we understand, "Oh for this moment I'm seeing. For a moment I'm hearing. For a moment I'm thinking." It's a continual dance of the consciousness with the six sense doors. That is all we're doing.

But we begin to see that more clearly and recognize the phenomenal dance. Then we see what's true. What's true is that there is no actual stability. Because the consciousness itself is very much like a candle and the wax. Imagine a candle is lit and is burning its wax. From a distance it appears solid. But if we look close, we'll see that the candle (consciousness) and the wax (object) are igniting at tremendous speed moment after moment after moment.

This is really what *anicca* is. When we observe our thoughts, our smelling, our tasting, our seeing, our feeling, and our hearing, we are seeing an incredible dance that appears solid.

The mind is phenomenal. The mind is doing something that is actually not true. Its basis is to stabilize the form, the organism. Therefore, its nature is to hold things in captivity so that they appear solid. Then we buy into that solidity, because that is how our minds work. Then we feel safe. "The room is solid. The ground is solid. Everything around is solid." So there is a sense of safety. But it's not true.

That is where the practice comes in. It starts to feel and look into the subtlety of the impermanence. The Buddha said, "To see into the impermanence is one of the greatest happinesses." That is interesting. This is a counter-action to the nature of the mind. As soon as you recognize that all of this is just a shifting, moving experience, there is a sense of relaxation. "It's okay. It's all changing."

In my childish mind I would think, "I give up then. Forget it. There is nothing I can do here." But there is more to it and there is much more understanding that can happen.

The conditioned nature of the mind is to solidify, the nature of the truth experience is a dance of impermanence that is happening continuously. One of the unfortunate realities, because of impermanence, is that things have the nature to rise up and pass-away. We all have the nature to arise, and no matter how we arise, we are all going to pass away. I think even in that, there is a built in trance that goes with the mind. It doesn't believe that it will die. "Okay, you are going to die. I can deal with that. But me? No. I don't buy that. It's just a misconception. It's a bit of confusion." I think genetically it's also built into all of us.

Suffering (*Dukkha*)

So the truth is: we have refused to accept impermanence. When we do that, we suffer. And that suffering, *dukkha*, is the next fundamental characteristic. That's not the only truth and unfortunate reality. Not only are we impermanent; none of this is stable. It's all in flux. So what is it that we can feel safe within?

We feel safe when we solidify and hold on to things - a house, a car, relationships, or whatever.

But, there are no promises here. You can die tomorrow or tonight. It happens. We don't know anything. Because of the idea that we can somehow freeze or hold something because it's good, then it shouldn't change or pass away. But, unfortunately, it does.

And because it does, and because of the nature of our expectations of wanting and clinging, we suffer. The truth is that things arise and then pass away. When we prefer them not to work like that we suffer.

There are two levels with the suffering. One is because of time. Things arise and as time goes by, their nature is they also pass away. We are all passing away. Sometimes I get sad because it's not fair how it works. When I see someone who is fifty years old and dies of a heart-attack, I think, "They are in the prime of their life. Hey, wait a minute!" There should be some kind of big daddy who takes care of this. But this is actually random. We don't know. We begin to understand there is a component of suffering, which the Buddha said I can't do anything about. That component is time. When something arises, it has a certain period and then it passes away. That is a specific kind of suffering.

But there is another suffering, a suffering that we are more interested in. It's actually much bigger for human-beings. This is the suffering of our attachments. In our attachments to our bodies, our attachments to our views, to our opinions about everything, we are not open. Instead we solidify "this is the way it is".

Maybe you were taught, "This is the way it is," and you carried that on some level. You can make it just the opposite, too, but it's still the same thing. It's all based on this word *upadana*. *Upadana* translates into "clinging" - clinging for or against things. The results of that clinging is suffering.

With the insight practice, you look deeper and see the impermanence, and you begin to see the nature of suffering, and the components of how we create it and how we hold on. We can also see how we release it. This is such a fundamental piece.

No-Self (*Anatta*)

The third of the obvious Characteristics is *anatta*, which is translated as "no self". But the

Buddha didn't really talk about self or non-self. I usually say, "Let's do a reality check here."

In the tradition we talk about the two truths. These two truths are the relative and the absolute.

From the relative point of view, and this is a lot of surface material, you exist and you walk around in the relative world, and we are relative neurotics. We stumble around with our unknowing. And we freeze our beliefs in time.

The absolute, which is the other side of this, is what the Buddha was more interested in. Ultimately, you are just a multiple-personality. Anytime you meet a new situation, you are a little different because of the impermanence. Sometimes you abandon yourself. Sometimes you attack. Sometimes you attach. In that multiple part, there is also a greater truth.

That greater truth is that from the ultimate or absolute point of view you are everything. It's not that you are not a something; you are everything. This is kind of cool. You are going to have to play with the pieces. They are two truths.

The Buddha called this the most essential part of his universal insights. He came from the

Hindu religion with its idea of *atman*, the permanent self.

Goenka once described the *atman* as a sesame seed in a human being, which passes from life to life. The Buddha disagreed. His response was that the self is just a changing thing.

No, you are just a changing thing.

When someone asked, "What then is reborn?"

My favorite answer is from Trungpa Rinpoche, "All your bad habits, of course." It's the habitual that keeps going. I just love this; I have heard him say it so many times!

These three - *anicca*, *dukkha*, and *anatta* - are the basic Characteristics but now I want to drop deeper one more level. Dropping down to this level is something that is not taught very much, but I feel it is essential if you are to understanding the ultimate and non-dual awareness – this unconditioned awareness. I'll try to tie in these three Subtle Characteristics.

Simply Emptiness (*Sunnata*)

If we begin this process of investigating those aggregates and the impermanent dance that is going on, we begin to see that not only is everything impermanent, but it's empty of any inherent existence. We imbue form on things. That is how we solidify the impermanence on some level. We make it solid. But from the level just below is where the word "emptiness" or *sunnata* comes in.

This is a difficult word and I think a good word. I'll try to clarify that. It's a difficult word, because in our culture, in the early translations they used the word "blankness". In our language the word "empty" was a negative that said, "No." But that is not the exact meaning. When you read the other translations, there are many cultural understandings of this very essential Buddhist concept. It's not about blankness.

Really, it's about our infinite potential. When we breakdown impermanence into its elemental components, it has no inherent existence. We know this from physics and chemistry. We only impute meaning and form on everything.

Through our seeing, our smelling, our tasting, our hearing, and our thinking, we impute meaning. But we can break it down. We can define what it's not, which is one way of doing it. I like to think, "No, it simply means that you have released it and it has infinite potential to arise as anything."

To me, I like this way of looking at it because I don't need to re-empower the objects. I see them in their separate molecular form. It's not something I need to attach to. It's something I need to note and something that has an impermanent nature and arises and passes away. Even the mountain has its time.

It's incredibly powerful to have trained your mind to see the emptiness. In essence, we are no longer attaching. You see form, but you're not buying it, you're not believing. It is substance-less. If it's substance-less you have the incredible power to let go. By seeing the emptiness, you can say, "I let go." Or, not even the "I", just "Let go". This is inherent in the insight.

The Is-ness of Things (*Tathata*)

If we just left it there this wouldn't be enough. You would have this emptiness and it would deny the world we inhabit. Therefore, the second insight, which comes from the awareness of suffering, is *tathata*, which is translated as thusness or is-ness.

What is thusness? Things are exactly as they are. In the Mahayana and the Prajnaparamita traditions they talk about the emptiness in form. This is the form. The form is the is-ness or the thusness of things. I'm not trying to change what's here. It's exactly the way it is and it all has its own nature. It arises due to conditions and it will disappear due to conditions.

There is a release where I can see through it. If it gets a little sticky, I know it's empty of any inherent essence so then I can let go of it. At the same time, "Oh, boy!" It's part of a relative reality and I'm in a thing called time. I'm in a thing called the aggregates of these forms; and along with this condition comes *dukkha* or suffering attached to that.

Emptiness has the power to let go. The *dukkha* (which goes to just the way things are - the thusness, the form) is where love is. It's where if one sees the inherent freedom of things, one also sees by their nature that all of it's going to arise and pass away. Even in the midst of the happiest wonderful situations, this too will pass away. This is like a reality check of "I see, when I'm in form, I'm in time. Everything I touch has this nature of passing away."

So there is natural understanding of compassion for the truth of this process. "I'm not separate from it. You're not separate from it. We are all in this together."

I hope you get this. These are the essential pieces of the deeper waters toward unconditional awareness.

Not-There with the Object (*Atamayata*)

The next subtle characteristic is the *atamayata*, which translates as "not there with the object".

We take the fact that there is no permanent, solidified self; we see that and see its nature; as you do with these other insights, and you come to *atamayata*. *Atamayata* says, "I'm not there with the object. I see, I hear, I taste, I feel, I think, but I'm not there with the object."

There's a self and there is the mind that goes to the object briefly. It's there for the eight moments and then goes on to another. But this is saying, "I'm not buying any of it. I release any attachment to the identification, to the duality itself." To be caught in the duality is not what *atamayata* is. *Atamayata* means, "I'm not going to be there with the objects."

Where do you go? You fall back on the unconditioned. You could say "just the unconditioned". It's simply an unconditioned awareness. It no longer holds anything specific.

In a sense, it has always been with you. It's not something you created or were ever separate from. You simply begin to see through the layers and come to this place that has released its hold on the wagon, on the *samsara*. It's not that anymore.

To go through these stages, it's not that you become something different, rather, you are free from. To be free from means that you are also in the middle of. But there is this undisturbed awareness that holds the space and has this phenomenal ease and love.

Get over yourself!

CHAPTER EIGHT

KARMA

An important aspect of this practice is *karma* (or *kamma*) and how we hold it. There are Five Daily Reflections that monks recite every morning and before sitting:

I am of the nature to grow old. There is no way to escape growing old.

I am of the nature to have ill health. There is no way to escape ill health.

I am of the nature to die. There is no way to escape death.

All that is dear to me and everyone I love are of the nature to change. There is no way to escape being separated from them.

My actions are my only true belongings. I cannot escape the consequences of my actions. My actions are the ground upon which I stand.

Here is another interpretation of the Five Daily Reflections:

I am the owner of my karma.

I inherit my karma.

I am related to my karma.

I live supported by my karma.

Whatever karma I create, whether good or evil, I shall inherit.

I think we have to draw back a little and start to tease out the words themselves. In the 1960s we had this word *karma* that came maybe into our awareness from the Beatles; and it evolved in a way that was misinterpreted.

There are actually two words involved.

- *Karma* simply translates as action.
- While another word, *vipaka*, translates as fruit or result.

- What we do is action, that's *karma*.
- What we experience is the result, that's *vipaka*.

We need to be really clear on that.

Karma has a complexity, and the reason it is complex is that it is a very modifiable thing. In the

1960s we had an idea that it was a fixed thing, when actually it's not mechanical in any way.

The Buddha taught us not get too wrapped up in it. He called it one of the four unthinkables. In a sense, it is something you have to explore and understand. He also said that you should reflect upon it every day.

There are two pieces here. One is not to try to look at a specific event and say, "Oh this happened because I did that." It's way beyond that. That is a simplistic idea. I remember in some of the cancer groups in the 1970s, there was a lot of confusion around *karma*. "Is the cancer my fault?" If you look at the complexity, it can't be that way. It is this phenomenal, multi-layer thing that happens.

I am going to give you some explanation from a Buddhist point of view, because from a Hindu point of view *karma*, mixed with *vipaka*, is a fixed thing, a mechanical process, the laws of the universe. The Buddha refuted that and talked about it from a different aspect.

The Buddha said the primary piece here is around intention. Intention is the baseline of how *karma* works. Consider your intention to be with your breath. How many times do we intend to be with our breath and then our mind wanders off? Shall we keep a scorecard and check to see how often this is happening in comparison of all the moments? But our intention is to stay focused on the breath, and the intention is what will reap the benefit of our action.

When you look at the word "intention", there is intentional and unintentional. Say for instance, there is the precept about not killing. You may be walking on the path up to the little lake and you step on an ant. In Jainism or Hinduism the mechanism of the laws of nature say that you will get the result of that. The Buddha said no, you will not get the result of that, you only get the result of intentional acts, which is really a great relief. It is a big thing.

There is a mechanical truth about reflecting on our actions. But there is also the intention, which influences the results.

What is also true about the mechanical part of this is that it is mutable, modifiable. If it wasn't modifiable, certain actions that we all have done in a long life, if they were part of a mechanical system, would mean we could never reach enlightenment. It would be virtually impossible. It would take eons and eons. To become a Buddha takes eons, but to become awakened, doesn't take so long. So *karma* is something that is very modifiable.

But, the process of result is kind of a mystery, too. We just don't know.

When the Buddha explained this, he talked about three aspects of it: mind, speech, and actions. He used the analogy of going down to the ocean. You write a word in the sand where the waves touch the shore. The next wave comes along and washes it away. That would be like a thought. You can think some pretty wild things and it won't necessarily have a result. With speech it becomes more concretized. There you go above where the wave touches the shore, and write you a word. A big storm has to come along to erase that speech or word. An action is like carving the word in stone in the rock wall along the shore. These are the thought, speech and action.

Why is this complexity here? We each have an individual mind-stream that's happening. In that mind-stream there are certain actions that occur. The way the Buddha described it was that if you perform a lot of generous and good acts and have been quite careful, your mind-stream is like the Ganges. If you add a teaspoon of salt to the Ganges, it isn't a big deal. You can't taste the change in the water. But, if you haven't performed as many good and generous acts, your mind-stream would be like a glass of water. Adding a teaspoon of salt to a glass of water would create a bitter taste. That is where some of the complexity comes in and the truth of the *vipaka*.

As you sit here, from the outside it seems that you're just sitting like a bump on a log. But just watching the stream of the mind and learning about *karma* and intentions and results, this helps build your intention. It is building for goodness. It is building to bring the mind back into being mindful. There are some very strong *karmic* results from that, more than you can imagine.

The Buddha said, if this did not exist, then there could not be the holy life. So there are things that we can do to modify our *karmic* existence or the *vipaka*. Whatever is following behind us, is mutable, is changeable.

There is a story:

A spiritual seeker went crazy trying to follow his teacher's ill-advised guidance and began living like an animal in the jungle. He killed people, cut off their little fingers, and wore them around his neck on a necklace. He was called the Angulimala, "the garland of fingers". He vowed to collect a thousand fingers. After he had collected 999 fingers, he encountered the Buddha, who was to be his 1000th victim.

Angulimala grabbed his machete and ran after the Buddha. The Buddha was not moving, but no matter how fast the Angulimala ran, he could not catch up. He finally yelled at the Buddha, "Stop."

The Buddha turn around and said, "Angulimala, I have stopped. When are you going to stop?" In that moment, whatever karma Angulimala had accumulated broke his psychotic state, and he changed instantly and soon reached liberation.

That's phenomenal. For us, whatever we've done is not a big deal. The story is not over, it goes on:

Angulimala walked through the villages where he had killed people and the villagers threw stones at him. He allowed that to happen. Finally, the villagers saw that he wasn't the same crazy person he had been. He was no longer a psychotic, he was one of the monks of the Buddha, one who had attained a level of liberation.

There is another story I will tell you. It is the story of Milarepa, who was Tibet's great saint.

Milarepa's aunt and uncle stole his land and threw him, his mom, and his sister out on the streets. With his mother's encouragement, he left home and learned the black arts of sorcery and magic.

Milarepa returned to his village to kill numerous people for revenge. He then met his teacher Marpa.

Marpa had Milarepa erect stone buildings and then tear them all down, over and over again, as a process of repentance and purification until he could understand the teachings. After he understood the teachings, Milarepa became Tibet's most famous saint. He was able, within one lifetime, to go from confusion and a truly distorted state to a liberated state.

That's really what we're working with here. We all have stuff that we don't know where it's coming from or when it's going to come. We have no idea. But, this teaching is saying, it is modifiable. If greed comes into your mind or revenge and you replace that with *metta,* or you do an act of generosity, or you respond with kindness instead of your usual reaction, the whole thing changes.

So we have the capacity, even though we may have to experience some difficulties, to change our *karma*. I think we all will have difficulties, it's a complicated world in that way. What we are doing here is creating or training a mind that can modify its *karma*.

It is sometimes described as having a lit candle. As the candle burns, the light we see is consciousness contacting the wax, which represents the six senses. That wax, as it burns, is due to the *vipaka*, to the result of our past actions that come up and are being burned. A candle, from far away, looks like a solid thing, like the self. If we look at the candle very closely, we see it coming up and igniting thousands of times every moment, just as consciousness touches each of our doors of perception. But the wax is what is actually pulling us along. It's our habits, our fabrications, and our sense of who we are.

A few years ago, I went back to Asia for a year. I felt I needed to study a lot. I spent a couple of months sitting in retreat at Bodhgaya then later in Ladakh. Afterwards I spent four months in Dharamsala studying with three different teachers. My interest was the writings of Nargajuna on the argument and analysis of "emptiness". This is a very complex argument, simple in one way and complicated in another. I also did the seven-point mind training with my main teacher there, Thrangu Rinpoche, who is about the same age as the Dalai Lama. I also studied a text called *"Cutting through Appearances"*.

When I returned to the United States in the 1970s after eight years in Asia, I felt like a stranger in my own country. I experienced a different kind of culture and practice from what I had been taught. I spent the next seven years studying psychotherapy and traveling with Jack Kornfield. Under his mentorship, I learned how to adjust to being in the West and how to teach in this different environment.

But there were some things we were hesitant to talk about. One was *karma*; another was emptiness and another was rebirth.

As part of my recent investigations, I ended up at Ladakh in the mountains reading texts about *karma-vipaka*. Based on my research, I want to attempt to explain a piece of it to you, in the only way I can describe it, given the way my mind works. Imagine you had five copper wires that could carry positive and negative energy and they all had plastic coating on them. These are the *karmic* sequence events that hold us.

The first wire is the order of the physical or the inorganic. That includes the time when you were born, longitude and latitude where you were born, the food that was available and what you ate, who your friends were, the political and social environment. It is really the physical world. This is one aspect of your *vipaka* and the reason we have a lot of similarity.

The second wire is the order of the organic. This is your genetic code, and includes your different propensities for seeing, inherited from your parents, your grandparents, your great-grandparents, etc. It also includes the traits and tendencies carried in your DNA, your physical appearance, your weaknesses toward drugs, and all the things carried as part of your genetic coding.

The third wire is the mind-stream. The mind-stream is a particular version of the candle wax, specifically what is carried by the individual. When my kids were born, for the first twenty-four hours, I could swear they were somebody else. Then they turned into a baby with a need of incarnating here. Maybe it's my imagination, but that being came in with something.

We can see this in identical twins, even though they have the same education and the same everything, yet they are so different. Why is that so? Certainly it is not due to the organic. This mind-stream is specific to each human being, to each individual who is here. It could be a child prodigy in family of bikers. It's the mystery of what we don't know.

This particular wire (the third wire) includes our personal habits, not just the collective. As for the collective stream, there are certain characteristics common within our environment and our culture. We are very fortunate in the order of the physical and in the order of the organic we've inherited in our collective stream, but the mind-stream is specific to each individual. Even with all our problems, but we're still very fortunate to have been born when and where we were. You may have experienced some very difficult things growing up, but you've all made it this far.

These first three wires are common to all of us. The next one is where I got really confused.

The fourth wire is translated as psychic life or order of mind. It is power of mind. This includes: telepathy, retro-cognition, and premonition as well as clairvoyance, clairaudience, and thought reading. Most of this is inexplicable to modern science. We are just learning little pieces about the mind. We might see results, but we may not know the parameters of it.

One of the things I read was that prior to a hundred-fifty years ago, in the order of physical, we would have lived in a much quieter environment. We wouldn't have had electricity. We wouldn't have had cars. We wouldn't have had so many things that support the material. These have become so difficult for the mind-stream. So maybe in earlier times, these psychic traits were stronger and more common.

In Jungian psychology, they say that up to 25% of dreams are precognitive. There is a premonition of forthcoming events. I don't know too much about it, only that it is available.

There are also different levels of concentration. The *jhanas* or the absorptions and the formless are really unknowable to the conceptual mind, but they exist and are part of this practice. In the time of the Buddha there was a lot of mind reading and magic that existed.

The fifth wire, which also took me a while to figure out, is that all beings have a basic goodness. That is also part of this energetic field that surrounds us. A lot of times we don't get in touch with this, so it is not readily available to us.

Next, let's look at what the Buddha did in this area of the wires. This is all my interpretation. The Buddha began to work on the mind-stream, the individual center copper wire. When he left home for six years of austerity, he began to thin out the insulation around that third wire. He thinned it out, which began to affect the fourth and fifth wires. As more energy went from his subtle mind-stream wire into his order of psychic mind and basic goodness wires, he finally reached a state where so much positive energy was running through these copper wires, the insulation melted and the wires fused together. Then the individual mind-stream of Siddhartha Gautama of the Sakya Clan suddenly had his moment of awakening. He melted his mind-stream, psychic mind and basic goodness wires together.

One thing that does not happen, the organic and the order of material (physical) are not melted with other three. That only occurs when the Buddha dies.

So in this process in the order of the organic, he went back to his family and his cousins and his relatives. They all followed him as part of the mind-stream and a majority of them became awakened, except his father who continued wanting him to be a king.

That fusing happened at the time of his awakening when he was sitting under the Bodhi tree. He had his enlightenment experience, then he began a series of reflections, which they call the second watch of the night.

After his awakening, he sat and began to reflect. You and I would call it a life review. For him, he called it a mind-stream review. He went back 900 lives and recounted the actual story of his many lives leading up to his awakening in what is known as the *Jataka Tales*. He had been an animal and a sailor and the king of the Nagas in Benares and many different things in his past. But what he established was the fact that this was a stream that was happening. His candle would blow out and then reignite again with the same wax.

Could this be part of this stream of consciousness? A lot of times we don't talk about this. Except, it was his own life review that the Buddha explored. If you were to believe his experience, then it says something to us. It says, first we have to be aware of the *karma*, and that the *vipaka* is unknown to us. This is something that goes on. It doesn't have to be a belief system. It can be a way of understanding - a skillful means of how we want to operate in our lives.

So, I'll tell a story of why this interests me. In 1968 I had lived in Europe and Paris and came to California to Haight-Ashbury in San Francisco. I ended up living in Boulder Creek in the Santa Cruz Mountains in a little cabin. At the bottom of the road from the retreat center was the little cabin I lived in. I still pass it all the time when I go there to teach.

I had just come from a twenty-four-day retreat and I got hepatitis. I was very sick but I had been thrown out of the Santa Cruz hospital because my friends were smoking pot in the corridor. I had no understanding of hepatitis and the liver. My friends would bring things like fried chicken and French fries, and I would eat it and then I would throw-up. I had been really sick for a few days. A lot of the problem was diet and confusion on how to take care of myself.

One particular night, I was in my cabin alone. The friends that I lived with were gone someplace, and I was by myself. I woke up in the middle of the night about two or three o'clock in the morning. It was in the wintertime and the window was fogged up. When I looked out the window, however, there by the creek, was a big man holding a black hat. I could see him as clear as day. I had no idea who he was or what was happening.

There was a strange sound that I thought was creek noise, but at a completely different rhythm. I later realized I was hearing chanting. I watched and listened for probably an hour wondering, "Am I awake? Am I asleep? What's going on?"

When I had gone to bed, my skin was yellow and my eyes were yellow. When I woke up the next morning, my skin was clear, although my eyes were still yellow. I went down to the creek, and I remember crying and wondering, "What have I done?"

Although I had hitchhiked up and down the West Coast, I realized I didn't know anything about America. About a year before I had come to Aspen, Colorado; and even though I was a ski-racer, I just didn't like Aspen. It seemed to me to be like "white bread and bad coffee". Now, however, it is terrific; but I just didn't connect with it then. I had been aimless, but that day at Boulder Creek, my life changed.

The next day a friend of mine came down from Berkeley and convinced me to move up there. A few months later, I was in London, after a flight with some "Beserkeley" kids. From there I hitchhiked across Europe to India. I knew something was pulling me, but I didn't know what.

I traveled overland and I got busted in Thessalonica, Greece. They thought I was a spy, because I had long hair and a peace sign on my backpack. I was placed in a straight-backed chair with bright lights on my face and grilled by guys in trench coats and hats. It was a scene right out of some grade-B movie.

Finally, I made it to Eastern Turkey. I was thrown in jail there, too. It was just one crazy thing after another, but I knew where I was headed.

Earlier that year my mother had died in a car accident in Italy. She had left me a little money and I was able to continue traveling. I ended up in Nepal that fall. I picked up a little funky pamphlet that explained how the emperor of China in the fourteenth century had a vision of a man wearing a black hat. The vision had healed the emperor of his disease. I read that pamphlet and thought, "This is interesting."

One morning some Tibetans came out of the mountains and the locals were having a black hat ceremony led by His Holiness the Sixteenth Karmapa. I looked at his picture and immediately recognized him as the man I had seen in the window in Boulder Creek, even though it had been a year or more.

My friends and I attended the black hat ceremony. When I walked into the room where the Karmapa sat, he immediately said to me, "Oh, I know you." He later became my first teacher.

At the time I thought it was spooky. I had never met a Tibetan. I didn't know anything about any of this. So what was this? I began then to see that there was more happening here than meets the eye. There is a lot more going on. This was something to give me inspiration so that I would stay on this path. All of the people who walked into that room that day were on this same path. There were four of us Westerners and three of us still teach today. One became a nun.

What does that mean? For me it is an affirmation that there is something going on here. What you are doing now is what helps me stay on this path of *Dharma*. There is no way I could have known. It wasn't part of the culture I came out of. I do believe that is how it works. I encourage all of you to stay with this practice. It is a refinement from life-to-life.

By the way, Buddhists don't believe in reincarnation, we believe in rebirth. You are not reborn in that sense. What you are doing is good and bad things for someone you haven't met and for whom you don't know yet. But you are a direct influence on that person and who and how they are going to be. That is part of the wax. This is serious. It is important to look at.

I know this is a lot tonight. But I wanted to try to explain it, although it is not an easy thing to explain. Hopefully, you got a little bit of it. It's not about the belief, but the understanding of your actions. You have the influence from your actions to change who you are. That's the biggest piece. You are actually free to do that. It doesn't say there won't be some wrinkles, but you do have that capacity.

I'll read one of my poems to end.

Sitting in Amazement

Oh, mercy, mercy, why sit in the dark with this pond of self,
only to dive into the darkness, sinking deeper and deeper,
only to allow the face-paint, which was so carefully crafted,
to dissolve into swirling colors, somewhere deep down in the unknown face-paint smeared,
tattered clothes of young princes and princesses stripped to the bone.
One turns up where the rays of dawn over hills of Japanese calligraphy
streaming colors shining through the transparency of our thoughts.

Next moment, crashing to the surface, dripping from the depths,
one looks down seeing the paintbrushes.
You, you, yourself, reflected on the water.
Jars of paint with names like mother, father, expectations,
old wounds, betrayals, beliefs, abandonments, fears,
all waiting to be painted back on that smeared face,
knowing somewhere, deep down, that less paint is needed to face the world.

CHAPTER NINE

THE WHEEL OF DEPENDENT ORIGINATION AND THE LIBERATIVE WHEEL OF DEPENDENT ORIGINATION

Tonight will be the obligatory talk on the Wheel of Dependent Origination (also called, Codependent Arising). The Buddha called this the crux of his teachings, as are the Four Noble Truths, which I began with the first night.

From the Buddha:

Profound, Ananda, is this dependent arising. It appears profound. It's through not understanding, through not penetrating this law, that the world resembles a tangled skein of thread, a woven nest of birds, a thicket of bamboo and reeds. A man does not escape from the heavy emotional realms of existence, from the states of woe and perdition and suffers from the rounds of rebirth. This not understanding of dependent arising is the root of sorrows experienced by all beings. It also is the most important of the formulations of the Lord Buddha's enlightenment. For a Buddhist it is therefore most necessary to see to the heart of this for oneself. This is done not by reading, nor by becoming experts in the scriptures, nor by speculation upon one's own and other concepts, but by seeing dependent arising in one's own life, by coming to grips with death through calm and insight into one's own mind / body. He who sees dependent arising sees the Dharma.

The Wheel of Dependent Origination

That is a good introduction. First and foremost, the Wheel of Dependent Origination (or Co-arising) is past, present, and future.

The past is pretty simple. Where there is ignorance, then the Wheel exists. Of course, ignorance is from the past, so it's multifold. If ignorance exists, then volitional formations, also known as *karmic* formations, come into being. As the Buddha said, "From beginningless time we have been trudging through [these lives or habit patterns and this follows you all the way along]."

We are such a mix of heavy/difficult and light/wonderful volitional formations. I have traveled the world and have seen the difference of just being born in the West, no matter what difficulties you have been through. It is a testimony to the positive actions that have brought you into this time and place. I believe this is an incredible time to be born as a Westerner and to encounter the *Dharma*.

The other night, I mentioned a centuries-old prophesy from Padmasambhava called, *When the Iron Bird Flies in the Sky, the Dharma will be Carried to the Land of the Redman.* I believe everyone here has some thread, a *karmic* or volitional formation, pulling you along. You may have some very hard times, but that is also part of the formula that brings you to this.

Once there is ignorance and there are *karmic* formations, then the next five links are based on the appearance as a human being. To be born human is a fortunate birth, by the way.

First, there has to be rebirth consciousness. Consciousness due to *karmic* formations, as we know in our experience, arises in the birth process. It's incredibly fickle. It's constantly moving at phenomenal speeds. It touches the sense doors as they happen. In the human condition, there has to be the rebirth consciousness, which is being reborn every second.

If it's being reborn, then it needs something to be reborn into. So there is a mind and a body. If there is a mind and a body, then there are the five sense doors and the mind. Then they appear in the human condition. If those six senses exist, they must have contact, and if there is contact there is feeling. Contact happens in the moment and we enter into present time.

In Buddhist psychology there are three fundamental flavors of feeling. They are:

- Pleasant,
- Unpleasant,
- Not-Pleasant / Not-Unpleasant.

When feeling happens, then the instinctual process of ignorance's first inclination is to grasp, either liking it or disliking it. As it grasps, then a series of sequential events occur. With grasping comes attachment. As attachment arises, then the moment moves into becoming, the ninth link in the Wheel of Dependent Origination. Becoming is a volitional formation. The grasping and attachment that happened due to the feeling then moves into the future, which become the tenth, eleventh, and twelfth links. There is birth, followed by old age, sickness and death.

That is the Wheel of Dependent Origination. I will go through it again, because there are a lot of steps.

There is ignorance.

When there is ignorance, there are volitional or *karmic* formations.

When there are ignorance and volitional formations, there is the arising of rebirth consciousness.

Rebirth consciousness, even though there may be a moment where the mind/body begins, continues through to the death of that being.

Right now there are certain conditions that bring this moment into being. In some ways there is the individual, which is part and parcel to those volitional or *karmic* formations. There is always an individual part happening and a collective that is going on. I don't want to confuse you on this. It's something that is mitigating the individual. You're not a fixed thing in this Wheel of Dependent Origination. You're something that has a past that is creating the present that is influenced by all the conditions of the present.

To me, the fact that you are being here with the intention of steadying yourself and trying to understand and have insight into all that there is, this is your own story. But the Buddha was not interested in your personal story. He was interested in your getting below the story to these universal principles common to all of us.

If someone comes here knowing nothing about any of this stuff, they just sit here in this room, with whatever individual piece that got them here. But, there is a collective force here affecting them. To me, that is fascinating. It's one of the reasons I started going to retreats and one of the reasons I like teaching retreats. I know that the individual *karmic* contraction is modulated or changed in conditions like this.

There are so many things you could be doing that would be part of that Wheel of Dependent Origination, which is based first on the volitional formations to that consciousness, with all its complexities, to a mind/body, from a mind/body to having the six senses.

With the six senses there is contact with the world.

With the contact with the world there is feeling.

With the feeling, if there is ignorance or confusion, then there is grasping, attachment, becoming.

All of this leads to birth, death, illness and suffering.

What I really am getting at here, and what the Buddha was saying, is that this is a map of dependent origination of how the past and being and the present and the becoming happen.

There is one place on the Wheel of Dependent Origination where we can get off. I think there are two, but traditionally we only talk about one.

First, if you eliminate ignorance, you step off the merry-go-round.

The other traditional place is with feelings arising as pleasant, unpleasant, or neither pleasant nor unpleasant. Since most feelings are not pleasant/not unpleasant often you are unaware whether you're sliding into grasping or not. When the conditions arise for the grasping, you can get off the Wheel just by noticing and returning to the breath or noticing the desire and bowing to it.

"Oh, I know you. I don't need to react to that. I'm simply going to sit here." Again, this isn't detachment, but nonattachment. "I am quite aware. I feel it and I know it. But I don't need it to be different than it is." This is an important statement. "I don't need it to be different than it is."

A lot of our practice is that things come up: discomfort, old memories, plans, or great stories. The ideal here is that somehow there are moments where we just say, "Oh, that."

It goes back to Ajahn Chah's teaching about being in the center of the room and staying in the chair. If you stay in the chair, and you don't go out through the window or the door and you actually stay, then you have mitigated, you have changed the situation.

This is actually a process of taking apart. We are taking apart the stimulus that comes to us and we're not reacting to it. Therefore, we are changing the *karmic* direction. This has the propensity and the power to change things. This is why we come to retreats. As we understand how this works, we see we have a choice.

You are all habitual creatures, who have responded to your experiences or thoughts or memories or sensations due to *karmic* formations. That isn't choice. That is just habit. We are pretty much habitual creatures.

Here we begin the process, not through doing, that is the trick here. It's through not doing anything. It's through seeing. It's through insight into the understanding of the grasping process. When we just stay in our seat, everything under the sun comes to visit. Things get very quiet.

My understanding is that there is the classic surface material, like a pond. We have created pontoons, which is a collective agreement at a retreat about silence, about non-harming, about the precepts, which are the fundamental protections here. We also get rid of our cell phones and all of our stuff, thereby blocking the majority of the stimulus from the outside. Then the material that is always being stirred at the surface is somewhat lessened, it's not so churned up. All these little things, maybe the body, memories, or health issues that keep the surface churning begin to settle.

We have to sit there for a while, and then we're at the next stage where we have dropped below it all. There is some complexity as we drop down. The *karmic* formations from the past, which are about the deeper, underlying material, can become the strong currents clouding the water. But we sit and allow the currents from the past to flow through, rather than throw us off course. They're not there forever. They're only a current. Their nature is that they arise due to past conditioning and they pass away. This relative side of the practice is a purification process. You are untangling or unleashing the habitual snares. This rouses us from our fundamental trances that we have believed in.

Sometimes after the waters have settled and become clearer, out of nowhere some little current will come along. It's compelling, it churns up the water and you think you're back on the surface and you haven't done a damn thing here. But, that isn't true. You are actually much deeper than you realize. Everyone here is at this stage, by the way.

At this point it's possible, if we're not jumping on the bandwagon of grasping and we are simply staying in our seat in the center and we have all the windows and the door open, that things can come and go without disturbing us. Even when old things come to pull us off the seat, we are here in this community that supports us to stay seated. So we stay in our seat. As a collective undertaking, this is incredibly powerful. We may get thrown off a little, but we come back to that seat.

Now we begin to see into our depths, the surface is all about I/Me/Mine. Our whole culture, with all the churning going on, is all about I and Me and Mine. That is all it's about. When you go deeper, some of the currents are the past I/Me/Mine. But the process is a purification process, an untangling going on. At some point, you can see deeper into the human condition, the nature of every one of us. We recognize not the separateness, but the non-separateness. That is what the Buddha was pointing to.

These deep, but simple laws, the simple *Dharma*, the simple truths that influence us all is what interests me. I love the three characteristics. I always mention them. I am constantly studying how they work, because I don't really get them. I know impermanence, but there are times when I have an insight into how ephemeral my seeing and smelling and hearing and thinking really are. I get a taste of it.

Sometimes, if I'm not looking too closely, it actually scares me, because what I'm looking at is the unstable truth of things, and it scares me from the I/Me/Mine perspective. From the universal, it's like "oh, that". This suddenly begins to breakdown the I/Me/Mine, that separateness that we cling to so strongly.

Even if you get rid of it for a moment, it reappears. It's really tricky and super smart. Suddenly, out of nowhere, some condition knocks us off center. When we get deeper we see these universal truths.

There are three *Dharma* gates that we go through. One is impermanence (*anicca*). In a deep, deep state we understand the truth of that, and we simply let go.

Another more difficult gate is suffering (*dukkha*). We observe the human condition at this deep level. Collective ignorance has repeatedly created this rebirth consciousness that is born confused, goes through life, suffers, then dies, only to do it all over again. That is the deep insight into the condition of suffering.

The third gate (*anatta*) isn't so common. "Who I think I am isn't who I am or what I am." *Anatta* indicates, "The self arises due to causes and conditions in a moment, but in the next moment it's not the same self. It appears to be the same self, but in this deep state, you realize it isn't. In a sense, the YOU seems to be same because of its *karmic* pattern, but it's not the same." That is an incredible insight.

These three gates are at the deepest level on the universal principles. Understanding them and the Wheel of Dependent Origination confirms that there is a place where freedom exists.

The Liberative Wheel of Dependent Origination

I want to do one more piece called the Liberative Wheel of Dependent Origination.

Suppose you are in your seat and you stay and you don't buy the jugglers and clowns and all the sense experiences and all the memories and planning and story-telling. You just sit there and be nobody. You sit and you're nonreactive. It isn't that you are not interested.

In the Five Aggregates there is the process of mental formation called concocting. The continuity of the self and time and future aren't there. You stay and you stay and you stay in your seat. Retreats allow you to get underneath the surface of things. As you go deeper and don't react, you see the suffering, the first piece of the Liberative Wheel of Dependent Origination. You understand that every time you jump on the Wheel of Dependent Origination through grasping, it ends in ignorance and suffering. This is a sobering insight towards liberation.

After you've seen that and decide not to return to the wheel, you make the effort needed to stay in your seat. You understand the conditions that will return you to the Wheel. You have *Saddha*, which is sometimes translated as confidence. But I see it as faith, and it's through faith that you've gone beneath the surface material and your faith is pulling you toward your own liberation. It's a simple thing.

At that point, you are staying in your seat, you are collected, you understand the nature of grasping. You are not doing anything with anything. You then enter these realms of joy, rapture, tranquility, happiness and concentration. These are the fruits of concentration. These are great experiences, many of which are quite transpersonal.

You could get stuck there for a while delighting in the joy and the delight and the pleasure. It's fun on a higher sensory level, but this isn't the end. I describe it as coming out of the pit of suffering.

"I know that there is liberation, although I can't see it yet. I have to have faith that I'm going in the right direction."

I think teachers can be helpful at this stage to keep you from going back to grasping, thinking "Maybe it'll work out this time." Actually, you have already done this millions of times. You don't go back. Instead you climb the next hill with faith, then you drop down into a pleasant valley.

Today I was thinking about the hot springs here. It was snowing. It was so pleasant. It was just beautiful. You could say life becomes very much like that. I know for me, when I returned to the chair, I longed for those pleasant states again. You have to dance back-and-forth until you get tired of it. After a while you realize those states really weren't as fancy as you thought they were.

Then you see another hill to go over and a mountain behind that. You leave this delightful little valley and climb to the top of the "the vision and knowledge of the way things are" hill.

"Vision and knowledge of the way things are" is a tremendous insight into the psychic life. I talk about the mystery of things and how we are creatures with blinders on. But when you achieve "the vision and knowledge of the way things are" the blinders are pulled back and you realize you have been inhabiting a teeny corner of the world.

You are suddenly open to the "unseen". We think of some occurrences as coincidences, but then we recognize the cosmic synchronicity of the knowledge and vision of the way things are. We recognize that is where we are. The only problem is that it's so fascinating you could get caught in the delight of the concentrations. You can get caught in the mystery of all of it.

But you still haven't gotten liberated. The Buddha knew all this. He would go into phenomenal states. He actually went to the highest states known. He experienced a lot of the cosmic realms, where he had his discussion about the "unseen" with *Mara*. But, he knew that was not enough. There was another mountain to experience. You have to abandon concentration to view the peak of complete liberation.

You see the world, and you see the transpersonal side of the world. "Oh," you think, "a lot more is going on here than I recognized." *Karmically* there is a synchronicity occurring that I notice sometimes and other times I don't. But it's happening nonetheless. In the shamanistic world you just left you were enamored with the unseen and the psychic phenomenon of the human mind and its living potentials. But you became disenchanted with that and realized you were not free. The Buddha was about six kilometers from the Bodhi tree, when he understood he wasn't going to achieve enlightenment through austerity or seeing into the unseen. He then resolved to confront the ten *Maras* and sit until he awakened.

I don't like the word "dispassion" as the translation for *viraga*, although some other teachers do. I think *viraga* means we became so enamored by the mystery of things that we can become satisfied. But in our practice, we return to our seats and understand we are not done. We think, "I know as much as I need to about the mystery of things. It is the way it is. But I myself am on this journey and I need to move ahead up this mountain that I recognize as the portal to *nibbana*, to liberation."

At this point, as you start up the mountain, there is a moment of emancipation or liberation. It's the first seeing into *nibbana*. When that occurs, some people are satisfied to stay there. But there are, in the tradition, four stages of *nibbana* and you can't get it all at once. You have to awaken in increments because the process is actually the breaking down of how we see things and how we experience ourselves.

To me, this is an interesting piece called "Knowledge of Deliverance", which means you've experienced the first gate of the four stages of liberation. Although you have only reached the first gate, you are not unconscious. You are aware that you have broken the trance of the human condition. You are no longer fooled by the idea of a solid self. You understand the transience of it all.

You also see how you have been a creature of socialization, of your family, your schools, and everything. Another way of looking at that is that you move from being a colloquial to a world citizen. You are suddenly no longer limited by your cultural conditioning. You actually know what has happened.

But, that is the precursor for these other stages to follow. In your journey up the mountain, you have to release each preceding stage as you move to the next. There is an effort involved in letting go of one thing and understanding there is more to go. Eventually you reach a state of *nibbana*, of *arahant*. That is the whole path.

But you first have to understand this entire Wheel of Dependent Origination to get off and stop the endless cycle of rebirth. At that moment of feeling, which only happens in the present, you can either keep circling or you can get off. I hope you each decide that in little increments that you're getting off The Wheel of Dependent Origination or Co-arising. It just incessantly goes around and creates this long process you have to go through to reach liberation.

I hope you understood pieces of this. If you didn't, that's okay. Just keep doing this. It's alright! You don't have to get it all at once.

The other night I read you a piece by Shabkar. Here is another piece for you.

Now come up close and listen. When you look carefully you won't find a mere speck of real mind that you can put your finger on and say, "This is it." And not finding anything is an incredible find. Friends, to start with, mind doesn't emerge from anything. It's predominantly empty. There is nothing there to hold onto. It isn't anywhere. It has no shape or color and in the end has no place to go. There's no trace of it having been by. Its movements are empty, but its emptiness is apparent. In the beginning, mind itself isn't created by causes and finally isn't destroyed by external conditions. It neither grows nor gets stuck. It's not empty or full. In choosing peace or anger alike, it shows no preference. Ceaselessly, it reveals itself as everything. So you can't say, "It's here." Not being fixed as something, it's beyond presence and absence. It neither comes nor goes, gets born nor dies, illuminates nor obscures. Mind's nature is vivid as a flawless piece of crystal, intrinsically empty, naturally radiant, ceaselessly responsive, strict bearer of samsaric error. Mind itself is always Buddha.

Chapter Ten

Cultivated Practices

I want to explore four fundamental aspects of the Insight Meditation Practice. We had many choices of which spiritual practices to bring to the United States from Asia, what would work and what would be useful for this culture. I want to briefly talk about these four.

- One is generosity (which is probably the most fundamental practice),
- The recognition of the Truth and the power behind ethics,
- Meditation as a series of steps, and
- Ultimately, loving kindness or *metta*.

Dana

The first, *dana*, simply translates as generosity. Generosity is a cultivated practice, as are all these four. Cultivating *dana* reminds me of my time in Thailand and going to the monasteries. One of the essential parts of these visits is the visitor buys a bucket of stuff wrapped in cellophane for about sixty-five cents. (It's a funny thing to watch, but I do it.) Then you offer the bucket to the abbot or to the monks.

The whole idea is that you are cultivating a practice. You are going to the monastery to practice *dana* that will then filter out into the community and into your life.

And, it works, by the way. It's not about the price of the gift. The giver is learning to loosen his/her grip.

This is a primary lesson when you go out there. It doesn't have to be an expensive gift is what I'm trying to say. But it needs to be something. Sometimes teachers say, "You may forget everything that you heard here. It went in one ear and out the other. But every day, as part of the cultivation, you mindfully did something for someone else, that is all, and you did it with the spirit of generosity and kindness. This is the fundamental cultivation that will lead you back to what this is." I could talk forever about this. These are the first teachings of how to let go.

The Thai are really generous people, but this practice is about the cultivation of the offering. I hope that if everything else goes, you understand this as primal. It's the first way to let go of clinging. I always find it wonderful to watch the parents teaching their little kids. The mama takes a ball of rice and puts it in her baby's hand, then there is a battle to get the baby to let go. The mother is insistent that the baby has to let go of this ball of rice into the monk's bowl. This cultivation of *dana* begins very early. I love these people.

You see this mother-baby teaching in Nepal, you see it in Burma. It's a trained practice. It's not about how much, it's about the mind seeing the nature of letting go. That is a primal piece. Sometimes, I think I can never say enough about this. You have to practice generosity and live it on some level. To let go of the story, to let go of yourself, to let go of your mind takes a specific kind of cultivation. Otherwise, it becomes a project. But this is a simple cultivation. This one piece.

Precepts of Non-Harming

Next, another primary piece is the precepts. The precepts are more about restraint, restraining from harming or killing.

Respecting life, all points of life, is fundamental and the first precept. All life wants to live itself. Our job is to protect and not harm and recognize that we are human beings, neither good nor bad.

In Asia, you have mosquitoes. The mosquitoes in the U.S. are very aggressive, but the mosquitoes in Asia are not as aggressive. Asian mosquitoes also like the color red. In Asia I sit over in the corner and wear a white scarf over my face, and they come and hang out on the white scarf. I had to go through a training internally. "They are an annoyance. I want to swat the suckers. Restraint—they have a right to live out their lives without my interference." It was a great training. Later on, I could see how it extended to other beings.

The second precept is so important in the world; it has to do with not taking what is not given. With possessions there is clinging, with clinging there is fear and non-ease. In a community that adheres to "not taking what is not given" as a principle, you can leave stuff out, and it will be there when you get back. That is in itself a tremendous gift. It's about feeling safe. My intention at retreats is making sure that the community has an identifiable sense of safety.

The third precept is about sexuality, which is incredibly powerful. Sexuality is a wonderful part of human relationships, but it also has a shadow side and complexity to it. Because there is so much shadow material around it, this is about safety. We restrain ourselves at retreats from any expression of sexuality.

I used to think that a sexual experience would be great as part of the spiritual experience at a retreat. But I would always stop and think, "Wait, what am I doing? No, I'm not going there." This is really important. I've been doing this practice for a long time. I've heard the stories, I know what people hide around this stuff. I've had to hear it. I understand the complexity of it and the importance of keeping it as simple as possible in our environment.

I also hope that you take this awareness out into the world and recognize that everyone has commitments and how they hold those commitments. I'm not saying this because I really understand this. This is complex. But it's again the premise of "not to harm" and how you hold the world of not harming.

The fourth precept concerns the world of speech. First, just understand speech! If you can keep your mind in your body, you slow the process down and avoid going into your head and back to your old babble. You first go into your body, then recognize exactly what your intention is in speaking.

The Buddha gave five suggestions. But if I can't remember them, I can just stay in my body and go to my heart. Then I know what I'm going to be saying, and I'm doing okay. The Buddha's five guidelines begin with, "Is it true? Is it kind? Is it helpful?" Also avoid negative speech, or harsh speech, or divisive speech or passive-aggressive speech, repetitive or controlling speech. We can all recognize these. The fifth suggestion on right speech is "Is it timely?" Is this the right time? We have to be sensitive to timing with our speech. At the right time, speech can help people awaken, or at the wrong time, it can cause tremendous harm.

The fifth of the precepts addresses intoxicants. People who are addicted to intoxicants and want to pursue this practice must completely abstain. I understand how difficult this can be. There are others who can consume intoxicants carefully and with moderation. I'm not saying either way is the only way, you choose how to deal with this. But we also know that in the family systems of almost all cultures, intoxicants have created a mess and caused great harm. But whether you need to completely abstain or consume in moderation is your choice.

So these are the precepts of this practice. They are restraints. One of my first teachers in this practice was Anagarika Munindra. I was about twenty-three years old, and thinking, "Come on. Give me a break. I don't want to hear about restraints."

He said, "You don't understand. If you follow these precepts and be precise with these precepts, your mind will not generate. If your mind doesn't generate, you can easily concentrate."

That sounded worth trying. It gave me a reason to accept the teaching, instead of blindly obeying some restriction from Bible class. This made sense to me. If I follow the precepts, then my mind is quiet; therefore, I can do this practice of cultivating this thing called meditation. These are the foundational pieces.

Meditation

When I came back to the West, all anyone wanted to talk about was meditation. They didn't want to hear about these other things that are the heart of the cultivation of the practice like generosity and the restraint of non-harming. But I think meditation is like the *mandala* in the center of the room. It's really nice to have a place that you've set up where you can go and cultivate a sitting practice. I like having a little altar, a Buddha, and a few things set up to remind me. It's also a place that you empower through repetition. You sit there every day, and it becomes like your temple. You empower that spot in your house. It's a wonderful part of this practice.

Then there are levels to the practice that I spoke about. Fundamentally, at times when there is a lot of chaos in your mind, *mantra* is just perfect. That kind of repetition and holding yourself within that world doesn't allow the mind to generate. It also calms you and allows some of the feeling base to be stabilized with equanimity. There are many stabilizing and collecting practices. The first couple of years of my practices I used *zazen* of the Zen tradition, which translates as "just sitting". I did time-travel thinking too much, but I didn't know not to. But it still worked. I calmed down some. I think it worked really well on one level.

Then I came to these Mindfulness teachings. For my Western mind, these were better for me. I start with the breath, then go to the body, then realize the power of feeling, recognizing and labeling emotions. I stay aware to not jump on the train of association. If you can do that, that is the practice.

But every day is a little different. Some days you sit down and everything is just completely calm and at ease. You sit down, you're with the breath, and then you relax into a peaceful and easy place. You can relax in that peace and ease and then open up to a wider venue. Other days, it's a busy, busy mind. When you sit down you need a technique to bring the system into a collectiveness. Sometimes it's a *mantra*. I think it's always good at the beginning to do a few minutes of *metta* to bring proper attitude to yourself. Whether the struggle is with emotion, some big plan, or a disturbing family memory, hopefully, you become okay with whatever it is and then settle down.

We call this insight practice because all these preliminary pieces lead us to seeing into our conditioning. That is really insight practice.

To see into your conditioning is seeing into and recognizing the truth of impermanence. It's of great value in learning the fundamentals of letting go and realizing that stress and suffering and discomfort come as part of being here and being human. Just acknowledging that and recognizing that this whole movie that you are starring in, and which appears to be so personal, is actually an impersonal process. That is such a great insight. It appears that I am caught in life, but if I look a little closer there is a tremendous amount of space of who and how I think I am.

When you have settled and you have space and you've gained a little understanding and insight into how it happens, then, sometimes, you have this ability - it doesn't have to happen all the time and it can only happen for a moment. You have the ability to step back, become aware of the sky or the ocean, and release the clouds and the waves and sit in the center of this marvelous world.

Metta

The last piece is about *metta* of the heart. When there is insight and the mind-heart releases its contraction, there is this natural heart, this natural goodness that is you.

I hope you will find a practice that fits you. I see this as a natural part of who you are and how you are when you're not caught.

I'm going to end with that note. I love the being part of it. Sometimes it's important to use phrases when you're a little caught. At other times, it's really just relaxing and feeling the heart and seeing there is the space to feel it and to respond to all of it in here and out there.

ABOUT THE AUTHOR

John M. Travis is the Guiding Teacher and founding teacher of Mountain Stream Meditation Center. He has been a student of meditation since 1969 and his vision and teaching have been very important in the growth and development of Buddhism and meditation in the Northern Sierra Nevada region.

John spent many years with recognized Asian Buddhist masters. He took Initiation with His Holiness the 16th Karmapa, who then became his primary teacher (Tibetan Buddhism).

John also studied with Lama Thubten Yeshe and later with the Venerable Kalu Rinpoche. He traveled to the ashram of Bihar School of Yoga under Swami Satyananda Saraswati where he took full Hindu monastic ordination for a short period.

In 1970 he began his studies in the *Vipassana* tradition with Anagarika Munindra and later becoming a student of S. N. Goenka.

John had the opportunity to travel with Baba Ram Das and to connect with Maharajji-Neem Karoli Baba. In 1979, John took full monastic ordination under the Venerable Taungpulu Sayadaw.

In 1986, John began teaching at a weekly meditation group in Nevada City, California, USA. From 1989 to 1993, John devoted himself to Senior Teacher Training with Jack Kornfield at Spirit Rock Meditation Center. After completion of his training he was ordained and given *Dharma* transmission in the *Vipassana* tradition of Mahasi Sayadaw and Ajahn Chah, and authorized to teach *Vipassana*. John still works here as a senior teacher.

He co-founded Mountain Stream Meditation Center and has a private practice as a meditation counselor. John has also trained in Hakomi body-centered therapy and Alchemical Hypnotherapy. He travels extensively, leading retreats all over the United States.

Over the last decade, John has co-lead a number of pilgrimage trips to Buddhist sacred sites including "In the Footsteps of the Buddha" - birth, enlightenment, teaching, and death - in India and Nepal, with a pilgrimage to Mount Kailash in Tibet.

During the year 2006, John lived in Asia and spent some of that time with His Holiness The

Dalai Lama in Dharmsala. He also spent time in solitary retreat in the caves of Ladakh. He continues to travel to Thailand, India, and Nepal and studies with Buddhist teachers or in retreat.

John M. Travis at the ruins

I AM GRATEFUL TO THE PEOPLE WHO MADE THIS BOOK POSSIBLE

Editing these talks has been a privilege and a challenge. Having an opportunity to listen closely to John's teachings again and again helped me better understand the Buddha's insight into relieving suffering in my daily life. This has been a great gift. Listening to a recording of John's talks, however, is not the same as sitting on retreat with him. Much of John's teaching is imparted through direct transmission; sitting in his presence during a talk conveys a deeper meaning than watching the same talk on a DVD. Recreating that level of understanding with the written word is near impossible. That is the challenge.

Recognizing the Truth in John's teachings, I knew I had to at least try to preserve his gift and do my best to pass it on to others who were not present at his retreats. Any misunderstanding or confusion with reading the preceding pages reflects my inability to adequately convey John's profound teachings and should not be interpreted as a shortcoming in his message.

To paraphrase the old saying, "It takes a *sangha* to produce a book of John Travis's *Dharma* talks."

First, I'm grateful to John for allowing me to edit and prepare his talks for publication.

Second, thank you to Tony Seikel and John Douthit who spent innumerable hours recording, editing and preserving these talks that could have been lost forever. And thank you to Steve Solinsky for his beautiful photographs.

John Travis also wanted to include a chapter on *karma*, but the original talk had apparently been lost. I sadly recounted to my wife Lori that the talk was gone and she replied, "Oh, I attended that retreat ten years ago and have a copy." So, she is responsible for our being able to include Chapter Eight and I am grateful to her for that and for so much more.

Dharma teacher Heather Sundberg and Community *Dharma* Leader Mary Helen Fein reviewed the drafts for content and form. Each of these people played a vital role in making this book possible. I'm deeply indebted to them and also to Mountain Stream *sangha* for providing a platform for many of John's talks and for accepting my wife Lori and me into this spiritual community.

Coy F. Cross II, Editor

IMAGES

Photograph courtesy of Steve Solinsky (2012)

Photograph courtesy of Steve Solinsky

Photograph on the front cover was taken at the Mountain Stream Meditation Nevada City Insight Center (2019)

ENGAGE WITH JOHN M. TRAVIS

John M. Travis on Facebook

https://www.facebook.com/john.travis.1069020

John M. Travis on the Web - For more information about John Travis and his pioneering spiritual work visit Mountain Stream Meditation's website: https://www.mtstream.org/our-teachers/

Please look for audio and video files of John's teachings in the Mountain Stream Meditation archives.

MOUNTAIN STREAM MEDITATION
NEVADA CITY INSIGHT CENTER

Whether you're new to Mountain Stream and Insight Meditation or you're an experienced meditator – everyone is welcome!

Mountain Stream offers a broad range of programs, classes and one day retreats to meet our community's interests and practice needs. We also host residential retreats at various venues two to three times per year.

Mountain Stream Meditation / Nevada City Insight Center is located at 710 Zion Street, Nevada City, California 95959

Website: https://www.mtstream.org/

Note: the picture on the front cover is of the meditation hall at "Mountain Stream Center", so in years to come, people who have never been there will still have a reference point.